Communication is Everything, Happy and successful through Intelligent communication

2017 – 2021 Paul Neuteboom / Communicatie is Alles
Illustrations and cover: Wilma Fransen & Paul Neuteboom
Translated into English by Suzanne Visser; Editor: Jonathan Smith

ISBN: 978-0-6456547-8-3

Published by Clear Mind Press in 2023 as Communication is Everything

Communication is Everything

Foreword for parents and teachers

I clearly remember the day that the idea for *Communication is Everything* came to me. We were sitting around the table – my wife Lisette, my daughters Lois and Isabel, and me. It must have been in 2007, a normal weekday. I do not remember what we were talking about, but I was trying to explain to my children how to have a conversation, just as my parents had taught me. I guess it had something to do with listening. Whatever I was trying to explain must have been simple, because at that time my daughters were eight and five.

After the children had gone to bed, I was sitting alone, staring into space. I thought how strange it was that there was no course on teaching children the skill of interpersonal communication, even though communication is such a big and important part of our lives. It's at least as important as maths and English.

The idea stayed with me. Over the years, I built up a collection of notes called "Communication is Everything". This was a phrase I sometimes used at work and at home. Whenever I had an idea or learned something about communication I added to my notes, with the aim of eventually developing a course on teaching communication.

A busy job and children who were growing up meant that the project did not make much progress. For a long time, it stayed on the back burner. Then, in 2017, I found the time to start working on it seriously.

The result is this book, *Communication is Everything*.

I am convinced that if we teach children to communicate effectively, they will have happier and more successful lives. My mission is to get lessons in personal communication onto the curriculum in schools. Children would experience the benefits for the rest of their lives.

I hope you enjoy reading this book and supporting your children in learning this important skill.

Good luck!

Paul

Foreword for students

This is a book that can help you get the most out of life.

It will teach you how to communicate as effectively as possible – with friends, with family, at school and in teams. This is important because good communication enables us to live happier and more successful lives. And isn't that something that everyone wants?

Our happiness is influenced by our relationships with our parents, our friends, when taking part in sports – in any situation. Communication is especially important for maintaining these relationships. If we are good at communicating, we are more likely to be happy.

Good communication also has a big influence on success in life. What do you want to grow up to be? A doctor, a road worker, a vet, a nurse, a firefighter, a plumber, a pilot? Whatever you want to be, you will have to work with other people. And working well together starts with good communication.

This is not the kind of book you have to learn by heart. Communication is not something you can get high marks for by studying hard, as you might for maths and English. Rather, it's something that you have to practise by doing a lot of it. You will continue to learn how to communicate well throughout your whole life. It is also important to remember that things will not always go smoothly. That is just not possible. We will all make mistakes, and the people we interact with will also make mistakes. This is how problems arise. Making mistakes in communication is just part of it.

But the knowledge in this book should enable you to make fewer mistakes. And if you do make mistakes, they should be easier to fix. I hope you really enjoy reading the book. Keep it safe and look through it once in a while, maybe after you have had a difficult conversation or when you can see a difficult one coming up.

Good luck!

Paul

In this book

1

Intelligent communication helps us to be happy and successful

Introduction

There are more than 25 million people living in Australia today. Many of them are happy, but others are not, or they are less happy than they could be. There are also many successful people in Australia, but that certainly does not apply to everyone in our country. Why is that?

Communication is an important factor in how happy and successful people are. That is why it is good to learn more about it and to get better at it. This book, and the lessons of the *Communication is Everything* course, will help us.

Let us first have a look at exactly what communication is.

Examples of communication

Pay close attention and you will see that communication is taking place everywhere. It is impossible not to notice it. Just think about a random shopping street near us.

As we stroll down the street, we see an elderly couple sitting together on a bench. They are eating ice creams and chatting.

Two girls are laughing while walking down the street, constantly checking their mobile phones. They are joking about the snapshots they have just sent one another.

A businessman gestures furiously, with his mobile phone to his ear. There seems to be a lot at stake, because he is turning red.

Above us, a flock of a hundred galahs is flying low over the houses. They are following one another as if they are tied together with strings.

A dog barks at its owner who is standing in the street talking to a friend. Probably he wants to run in the claypans nearby.

On the shop fronts there are billboards. They are trying to persuade us to do something. Oh yes, they are everywhere, trying to persuade us to buy those nice jeans, the cool earrings, or the latest magazine.

And as we get to the end of the street, we think about what we said to our best friend at school. Was that not a bit nasty? That is also communication – communication with yourself.

When we start to think about it – wherever we look, there is communication. We communicate in many forms and on many levels all through the day.

If we are good at communication, we can achieve a lot. Being less skilful at communication often has a negative impact.

Unfortunately, the latter happens too often. And when things go wrong, we are less happy and successful. That is a pity, because it is not necessary.

As we saw in the examples, there are many different forms of communication. The form we are going to talk about is personal communication.

Personal Communication

This book is about personal communication. This is, for example, the kind of communication we have with a friend or with a family member, when the two of us are talking about something.

Personal communication also occurs in a group. For example, in the schoolyard when we are with some friends. That is also personal communication, but then there are more people who take turns to speak and listen.

Personal communication is any communication between two or more people.

WhatsApp, Instagram and email are also forms of personal communication: through writing, video, audio and pictures. We will also be looking at these forms of personal communication. The number of messages sent via social media is huge. And things do not always go well there either....

The origins of communication

Communication began hundreds of thousands of years ago. There was no language, but there was behaviour. All sorts of behaviour. Think of a dog that is tilting its head. It is communicating: "do I get some food?", or "what do you mean?"

People also displayed this kind of behaviour a long time ago, through body language, facial expressions, and sounds. The sounds became more and more sophisticated. This eventually developed into something that we now call "language".

Scientists disagree about when exactly language was created. Estimates range from 40,000 years ago, to 150,000 years to 4,000.000 years ago. The fact is that language has been around for a long time.

Language gave us the opportunity to communicate cleverly. It is, in fact, incredibly special that we have developed language. Apes, dolphins, and whales may have language too.

We start picking up language when we are babies. About six months after we are born, we can already recognise between 50 and 200 words. When we go to primary school we already know about 10,000. By the time we leave it, we know about 40,000. The English language has more than 170,000 words, but don't worry - you don't need to know all of them to be able to communicate effectively.

Language enables us to express everything we see, hear, feel, and think.

From the moment we began to communicate, we humans explained to each other what we wanted from each other. We used language to reach our goals.

Many languages were created and communication through words became more and more important. How well we communicated played an increasingly bigger role.

Even then clever communication led to more success and happier lives.

Happy and Successful

We like to picture ourselves driving a cool car, being appreciated by our parents, living in a nice house with a loving partner. That is a beautiful goal. Everybody is entitled to a happy and successful life.

But not everybody has this kind of life.

It is important to ask ourselves why some people are happier and more successful than others. To answer that question, we must look at what happy and successful people have in common.

Good communication skills work

Research has shown that there is a correlation between happiness and success. There is also a correlation with being healthy. This is how important intelligent communication is!

Do you also think that intelligent communication can help you to be happy and successful? If the answer is "yes" you are not alone.

One thing that happy and successful people have in common is that they are good at communication. Good communication leads to healthy relationships, and healthy relationships make us happy!

Below are the elements of intelligent communication and their effects:

Element of intelligent communication	Effect
Being a good listener	People open up to us and tell us things People appreciate us
Understanding the people around us	We can help people We can motivate people
Knowing what we want and being able to express it in words	We make ourselves clearer to other people We are less uncertain, so we are calmer People respect us
Being good at building relationships and connecting people	This creates a peaceful environment and interesting relationships People want the best for us
Making friends easily	We have more friends There's help when we need it
Having more effect on the world	This gives us more control over our lives Some dreams can become reality

See how much we can accomplish with intelligent communication? And this list is far from complete.

The Chicken or the Egg

Happiness and success. One leads to another. Which comes first?

- Do we become happy because we are successful?
- Or do we become successful when we are happy?

Which came first, the chicken or the egg? Is this important? No! It does not matter. Enjoy the egg! Fry it, boil it, eat it hot or cold, but enjoy it! That is what we want this book to do. To teach intelligent communication, so that you can become happy and successful. And it does not really matter in what order, as long as you enjoy it.

Success means different things to different people

Most people think that being successful means having a well-paid job. But being successful means something else entirely.

Being successful = achieving our goals.

These goals can be very "normal" – such as learning how to play chess or to keep a soccer ball in the air a hundred times with our knees. Winning with our team, and collaborating with our classmates to get better marks, are all goals we can aim for.

It is important to know that being successful means different things to different people. Success does not always equal a big house, an expensive car, two butlers and a fifty-metre yacht. If that is our goal, great. But one goal is not better than another. What counts is that we become successful in the way we want.

Happiness and success not for everybody?

We may think that happiness and success are not for everyone. Some people may get sick or have an accident or are unlucky in other ways. If that happens, they are not happy and neither are they successful. But if we think that not everybody can be happy and successful, we had better think again.

The definition of happiness is different for different people. Some people with disabilities are much happier than people without disabilities. And some people who are sick are happier and more active than people who are healthy. Setbacks, in whatever form, do not have to stand in the way of happiness and success.

The scientist Stephen Hawking contracted motor neurone disease when he was 20 years old. Over time this made him immobile, and he ended up in a wheelchair. To communicate he had to use a computer that he found hard to control. This did not seem like a good basis for a happy and successful life. But he persevered, communicated and collaborated. He theorized about black holes in the universe. He became world-famous, successful and loved by many people, which brought him happiness.

Everyone determines their own happiness. The same goes for success. Sure, for some people life is disappointing. Yet intelligent communication also helps them to get the most out of life in terms of happiness and success.

Everyone has a voice

It is important that everyone has a voice and is heard. Why?

Firstly, because we will find ourselves having to collaborate with others a lot during our lives. For a school assignment, as a sports team or at work. Every member of a team should feel they are contributing. If people are excluded, it is more difficult to achieve the best result.

Secondly, the best ideas are sometimes born in the craziest moments. It may just be so that a classmate of ours is brooding on some great idea. If he or she never has the floor, in ten years' time we may not have that super safe flying bike that will take us to netball in two minutes. It would be a shame if we did not let such a genius say what was in her mind.

Albert Einstein, for example, was a quiet boy. He was not good at school and later worked at the archives in Switzerland. Yet, in 1905, he wrote several articles that would change the world. Without Einstein we would not have iPads, mobile phones, or GPS.

Summary

This book can change your life. If you use the ideas it contains, you will benefit for the rest of your life. Intelligent communication leads to better relationships with the people around you, and to happier and more successful lives.

2

The Communication Ladder

Introduction

In the first chapter we looked at what communication is. From this we know that communication is happening everywhere, all the time. Watching YouTube, texting our friends, a conversation with our brother or sister – all these are about communication.

In this book we are focussing on personal communication – because this is a skill that we will enjoy using for the rest of our lives.

If we look closely at personal communication, we will see that it works on different levels. This is what this chapter is about.

Knowing where we are

When we are in a foreign city, we need a road map. We need to know where we are to know where to go.

It is the same with personal communication. To reach our goals, we need to know where we stand.

When we are having a conversation with someone, we can suddenly find ourselves ending up in a shouting-match. This is like getting lost in a city we do not know.

And this is why it is important to recognise the levels of personal communication.

Levels of personal communication

Personal Communication contains four levels. They are listed below. Think about how they apply to your life.

Level	What we are doing
A chat	Sharing our stories
A dialogue	Sharing our opinions
A discussion	Trying to convince others
A shouting-match	Trying to get our way at all costs

The levels are ordered according to difficulty. Having a chat is easy. A dialogue is a little more complex. Having a discussion is difficult. And ending up in a shouting-match means a big breakdown in communication.

It is important to understand these levels and to recognise them. They show what to do and what to be aware of. An easy way to memorise and recognise them is the Communication Ladder.

The communication ladder

Imagine a ladder that gets narrower the higher you climb. Every rung of the ladder is a communication level. As we climb the ladder, it gets more and more difficult to stand on the rungs. The higher we climb, the further we can fall.

Let us look at the separate rungs, or steps.

A chat

This is the easiest level. It's just a chat with someone, or in a group. A large part of our communication is like this.

"Did you win at soccer?"
"How was your dance class?"
"Has your dad returned from his business trip?"
"Does your foot still hurt?" Etc.

A chat can go into any direction, and often does. One kid tells something about his soccer match; the next one carries on with a story about his tennis match. The next one mentions the terrible rain during her netball game. The next one asks where that rain came from – and before we know it, we are talking about rain. There is nothing wrong with that.

A dialogue

Sometimes a chat lands on one topic, because that topic is important or interesting. At that point it becomes a dialogue. The topic does not change any longer, and we exchange opinions on it.

In a dialogue we tell others what we think about a particular subject, but we do not try to convince others that our opinion is right. There is no problem if the other person has a different opinion.

We can recognise a dialogue by words such as:

* I believe….
* I think……
* My opinion is….
* If you ask me….

Later in this book, we will come back to dialogue, because it is such an important part of personal communication. But now let's move onto something a little more heavy: discussions.

A discussion

In a discussion we give our opinion and try to convince the other person that it is right.

This is where it differs from a dialogue. Everything is just a little more intense. This is fine, but it is good to be aware that you are in a discussion.

We can recognise a discussion by words such as:

* So that is….
* The truth is that…..
* It is a fact that…..
* It is clear that…..

Because we are trying to convince the other person, the tension is higher than in a dialogue. That tension can be tricky because we may say things we did not quite mean in the way they come out.

When that happens, we may end up in a shouting-match.

Shouting-matches

A shouting-match is a discussion with emotions. The emotions are so strong that we cannot think clearly.

Shouting-matches cause enormous tension and make us do things we do not want to do, because we are not thinking clearly. We may say things that make no sense, refuse to listen to the other person, or even use violence.

We can recognise a shouting-match by words such as:

* You do not know anything about it!
* How could you be so stupid!
* Get lost!
* Why can't you see that I've had enough of this!
  (along with all kinds of shouting and expletives).

After a shouting-match, you always have to make up somehow. After all, you cannot buy a new father, mother, sister, brother or friend. Making up costs a lot of energy and can take time. This is why it is better to avoid shouting-matches altogether.

Reaching your goals

Do we know why people communicate at all? Think about it.

On a basic level, people communicate to reach their goals. For example, when you ask your father if you can go to bed an hour later than usual. Or when a politician is trying to convince voters, or a teacher is trying to help us understand something. Or when a poet wants to move people. All communication has a goal of some kind.

It is important to realise this. We will come back to reaching your goals in a later chapter.

What does this have to do with the communication ladder? Well, it seems that the dialogue level is the most effective one for reaching your goals. This is why it is a good idea to use the dialogue level as much as you can.

We need to stay at the dialogue level as long as possible

It is important to remain on the level of dialogue as long as we can. We need to avoid climbing higher on the ladder to the levels of discussion and having a shouting-match.

The step up to a discussion happens like this: we are talking and agreeing and having a good time. Then, suddenly, we feel attacked and feel we must defend ourselves. Or we find ourselves attacking the other person. In doing this, we have gone one step up onto the discussion level.

This is because the urge to convince the other person causes tension in them. Something is not true or right just because we think it is. Other people want to reach their own conclusions by themselves. They don't just want to accept our view of how things are.

By simply presenting our opinion without wanting to convince the other person, we allow that person to reach their own conclusions. That makes them feel good – and it also helps us reach our goals.

A little bit of discussion and argument is okay

I am not saying that we should have no discussions at all. A clever discussion amongst friends can be fun. And we will have to learn to discuss things to be in a relationship, and at work. Discussions can be helpful to reach certain goals.

Even shouting-matches and arguments are part of life. Sometimes we fight over really small things. Why? Nobody knows. It is just the way things are, in a family, at work, at school or amongst friends. We cannot completely avoid it.

But we want to avoid discussions and shouting matches that prevent us from reaching our goals. So many discussions can be avoided. This can lead to shouting-matches and fall-outs, which cause people to distance themselves – in a team, between brothers and sisters, between parents and children, between friends…. This is really regrettable, and is really not necessary.

Summary

To communicate intelligently, we need to know where we stand. There are four levels of communication: chatting, dialogue, discussion and shouting-matches. If we learn to recognise these, we can adjust our communication accordingly. It is important to remain at the dialogue level as long as possible, as this is the best one for reaching your goals.

3

It's not what you say that's most important

Introduction

Yes, I know. The title of this chapter is a bit weird. This book is supposed to be about communication, but words are not the most important thing? Come on!

But you must have noticed often enough – even though it may sound strange – that sometimes you can say something, and it comes across all wrong to the other person. Even though you said exactly what you meant. What happened?

This is what this chapter is about.

Communication is not just about what we say

We may think we communicate with words. However. communication is not just about what we say – how we say it is at least as important. This is what non-verbal communication is about. That sounds difficult, but it's actually simple. Let me explain: 'Non-' means "not", 'verbal' means "to do with words".

Non-verbal communication is everything we communicate without using words – through our body language, our gestures, our facial expressions.

How does this work? Well, research shows that the actual words are not the most important aspect of our communication. The way you say something, and your body language, are more important than what you actually say.

Hard to believe isn't it? But this helps explain why communication goes wrong so often. Words, it turns out, make up only 7% of the message being put across.

At least 58% of communication is about body language, facial expression and posture. These are all non-verbal forms of communication – communication without words. You might say it's a wonder that communication works at all....

And 35% of your message depends on your tone of voice – how you say what you say. It is really important to understand how large an effect this has.

Now you understand why our parents get irritated when we say "Yeah, yeah" in a falling tone of voice when they ask us to clean our room. Next time, try just saying: "Okay, will do!" in a positive tone of voice and you will find there is less hassle.

If non-verbal communication and tone of voice are so important, how can we get better at using them?

How can we get better at non-verbal communication?

Improving non-verbal communication is not hard. We just need to remember that not everything in life depends on intelligence in an intellectual sense. To get better at non-verbal communication, we must use our feelings and emotions.

Question: Are your chances of a happy and successful life better if you are intelligent? Is the answer: "I am good at maths, English, geography, and history, so yes, I will be happy and successful"?

No, not in itself.

If we want to measure intelligence, we measure our IQ – Intelligence Quotient. This gives a score for how good we are at thinking logically. The higher our score, the better the chance that we are good at maths, English, memorising and analysing.

However, research shows that people with a high IQ are not necessarily happier and more successful. It turns out there are other skills that determine how happy and successful we become. These are the Social-Emotional skills – the SE skills.

Our Social-Emotional skills determine:

* How aware we are of our own emotions, and how we understand and control them;
* How aware we are of the emotions of other people, and how we understand them;
* How we adjust our behaviour to the emotions of other people;
* Whether we make decisions that are not only good for ourselves, but also consider other people.

The better our SE skills, the better we interact with other people and with ourselves. It turns out that good leaders often have highly developed SE skills. But I don't want to give you the impression that in order to be happy and successful you need to be in an important social position. I'm just pointing out that happiness and success don't depend only on IQ.

Let's not throw away all the maths books, though. We are not saying that IQ is not important at all. We are just saying that it is not necessarily the most important thing. Until the end of the last century, people tended to think IQ was pretty much all we needed. We now know that it's not, and we can use this knowledge to our advantage.

Good SE skills help us to communicate better, and by communicating better we develop these skills further. This helps us to have meaningful relationships with the people around us. And this makes us happier and helps us attain our goals.

The right mood, the right time, and the right place

Three other things make a huge difference in communication: the mood we are in, the time we decide to communicate and the place we choose.

In deciding whether the time, mood and place are right for personal communication, we are in fact using Social-Emotional skills. If we are aware of these three elements, our communication will improve.

Want to communicate cleverly? Be enthusiastic and cheerful.

It is almost impossible to react negatively to someone who is cheerful and enthusiastic. When we project that vibe, others will wish us well, in conversation or otherwise. This makes us happy.

Of course there will be people who will always react negatively, but they are a minority. When we are cheerful, the people around us also tend to be more cheerful. A cheerful vibe helps improve all non-verbal communication.

Of course, we cannot be cheerful all the time. There are days when everything seems to work against us. Even getting out of bed feels like an ordeal. On days like these we have to be honest with ourselves. If we recognise that we are not having a good day, we will understand that this is it is not a good day to engage in much communication, either. So it is probably not the best day to have that difficult conversation.

The next day everything often feels better, and we can face the world again and be cheerful.

The right moment

Discussions sometimes pop up suddenly out of nowhere, when we are not in the right frame of mind to engage with them, and that is where things start to go wrong.

For example, we might be on our iPad when our mum says something to us. She has a point and we know she is right, but because we are still wrapped up in the video we are watching, we do not give her the right amount of attention – and before we know it, we have found ourselves in a discussion, when a simple dialogue could have resolved the whole situation.

Nobody wants a nag for a father or mother, or a sibling, or a friend, but if they have a point and we value the relationship we have with them, we should give them the right amount of attention.

One way to make sure the timing is right for intelligent communication is to ask whether we can talk about it a bit later – in 15 or 30 minutes for example. This gives us time to prepare mentally, and the communication will flow better.

Tip for mum: she could ask us to put the iPad away for a minute, or to talk about things in half an hour.

The right place

Where our conversations take place also has an influence on their outcome. If the location is not right, it is nearly impossible to communicate clearly.

For example, if there is a lot of noise, it is difficult to concentrate. We do not hear the words well, let alone their tone. We become distracted and unable to pick up on non-verbal cues. A busy place is okay for a chat, but when it comes to engaging in dialogue it gets tricky, and having a proper discussion is impossible in this kind of setting.

Or it may be that the people in this environment are not the ideal company. This also affects communication. In this case it is better to delay the conversation or go somewhere else

Summary

The words we use are important, but what is even more important is how we say them. Our body language, and the tone we use, are also very important aspects of communication. These are influenced by our Social-Emotional skills. As we develop our SE skills, we will get better at communication. There are three other things that have an effect on communication: mood, timing and place.

4

Being clever about using smartphones and social media

Introduction

Smartphones and social media have had a massive effect on our lives. There has never been a technology that has had this kind of effect on us. Many people are engaged with their phones almost all the time. This, of course, has an effect on how we communicate.

Smartphones and social media

Most readers of this book (young people from 10 to 14 years old) have not known a world without smartphones and social media. But this world, as we now know it, is very new – everyone is still getting used to it.

Smartphones

Almost everyone now has an Android phone or iPhone. And people check their phones an average of 47 times a day.

Wherever we look, we see people with phones in their hands. The smartphone is a wonderful invention – a supercomputer that fits in our pockets, with apps that can do all sorts of things: take photos, record music, pay bills, record videos, play games, etc. It's no wonder that this gadget has become so popular.

Social media

Apps have made smartphones even more popular. The iPhone's App Store was launched in 2008, and was an instant hit. It now has two million apps available for downloading. Google's Play Store also contains millions of apps.

The most popular apps are the ones used for social media. Instagram, SnapChat, Facebook, TikTok, WhatsApp and more are all apps that help us stay connected to the world around us, including family and friends.

Nowadays we spend about three and a half hours a day on them. In 2010, that figure was about an hour.

Conclusion: our smartphones are wonderful computers which can keep us in touch with our friends and family seven days a week, 24 hours a day.

The downsides of amazing technology

As the famous Dutch footballer Johann Cruyff once pointed out, "Every upside has its downside." This is true of amazing technology as well. Here are some examples of technology with downsides.

Rockets

Rockets can be used to transport people and goods to the moon, and even to Mars – but as missiles, they can also be used as weapons.

Electricity

We use a lot of electrical appliances, and these are wonderful inventions. Even our cars are becoming electric. But generating the electricity to power these involves burning coal. This causes global warming. We need to find more sustainable solutions.

Robots

Robots are used to do things like building cars and going to places that would be too dangerous for people. Robots on Mars are making preparations for people to set up habitations there within 20 years. Fantastic! But robots also cause unemployment because they can work faster than people, are never sick and never complain.

Every technology has downsides – and this is true of smartphones and social media as well.

Smartphones, Social Media and Communication

We know that smartphones and social media have a lot of upsides. Here we are going to focus on four downsides, because these have an impact on how we communicate.

1. An overload of communication is unhealthy;
2. Screen communication leads to misunderstandings;
3. We live in a filter bubble;
4. Cowards for life (this will be explained later.)

Communication overload

The sheer volume of communications we receive is huge. We receive personal messages via apps such as WhatsApp, iMessage and Snapchat, and happily respond to them.

On top of all the personal communications, we have every form of media putting their latest attention-grabbing messages in front of us. Twitter, Facebook... they all do it, and without our being aware of it... it tires us out.

It is important to understand that apps are designed to grab our attention – not just a little, but a huge chunk of our attention. They do this in ways that can make us addicted to them. And once we are addicted, we have lost control.

As smartphones radiate blue light, this is especially a problem in the evenings. It means we cannot fall asleep and process all that information we have been exposed to. Our heads are too full to get a good night's sleep.

It is important that we control our smartphones, not the other way around.

It's a good idea to come to an agreement with our parents about how to manage our screen time. For example, not using our phones during meals and when doing homework, and not in bed. Alarm clocks are still available in shops.

If we do this, we will feel better and calmer. We will do better in school and communicate better.

Screen communication leads to misunderstandings

In the previous chapter we saw that body language and tone of voice are important elements of communication. Because these are both absent from screen communication, problems can easily arise.

Smartphones are, of course, excellent for exchanging short messages, such as:

"Could you get some milk?"
"I'll be there by 11am."
"Could you water the plants?"

It is great to be able to send these quick messages. They make things go more smoothly.

But for a real conversation the smartphone is less suitable – because there are elements missing. We do not hear the tone of each other's voice (35% of communication) and we do not see each

other (58% of communication). Emojis are not enough to express what we feel.

A smartphone is great for a chat, but not so good for a dialogue. And it is impossible to have a discussion on a smartphone – we should not even try it. The chances are that we will end up in a shouting-match.

We live in filter bubbles

A friend puts her birthday picture on Instagram. An aunt has just posted a fantastic photo of a sea turtle on the beach. Kim Kardashian is parading herself in another stunning outfit – while we are sitting at home doing our homework and thinking: "Why is my life so boring?"

This is caused by the filter bubble!

A filter bubble forms when social media shows us only part of the world.

It is important to know the two major causes of filter bubbles:

1. Algorithms (software) designed by large social media companies;

2. People showing only the positive parts of their lives.

Algorithms

The impact of algorithms on our lives is growing fast. For example, when one person types a search into Google, they will not get the same answers as someone else. Google matches its answers to people's unique profiles.

Facebook and Instagram also adjust their feeds to people's profiles – to what they click on, who they share things with and at what time of day. Every platform does this, to make sure we spend as much time as possible on it – because this increases its income from advertising. Every second we spend on Facebook or Instagram means big bucks for them.

The result is that Social Media platforms determine what our world looks like. This causes our filter bubbles.

Only showing the positives

When was the last time one of our friends posted a photo showing the dishwasher being filled? Or an aunt posted a video of herself vacuuming the living room? You practically never see this kind of photo.

On social media, people display their best moments: holidays, a nice walk, a party, a concert. Almost everything on social media is some kind of party. This is the second cause of our filter bubbles.

When we use social media, we should be aware of filter bubbles. If we don't, we will soon think that our life is boring and that we never do anything exciting. We will start thinking negatively about ourselves. This causes us to be less happy. Which is a pity, because everyone has highs and lows. The ratio is about 50-50.

A coward for life

We have all had the experience of receiving a text message that is not so nice. How did we feel about it? Not so good.

If this happens once, it is not a big problem. But if it happens on a regular basis, we are being cyber-bullied. This can have really bad consequences – not just for us, but also for the bully.

Cyber-bullying is cowardice

Cyber-bullying via a smartphone is really cowardly. Before smartphones, bullying took place in the street and in the school playground. When we were at home, we were in a safe place. We could think about what had happened and discuss it with our parents.

But today, bullying goes on 24 hours a day, seven days a week. It is extremely cowardly.

Anyone who wants to say something difficult to someone needs to do it face-to-face. This is a simple basic rule of good communication.

If we don't have the courage to do this, we should not send unpleasant messages in writing – especially not when we know that the person we are writing to will feel bad or insecure because of it. If we do, we will be responsible for their suffering, and we don't want that on our conscience.

Online lasts forever

Photos, videos, and conversations stay on the Internet forever.

This is especially dangerous for cyber bullies. They may think their conversations are safe in Messenger or on WhatsApp. But these platforms can be hacked. If that happens, their bullying will be there for everyone to see.

This can create enormous problems later in their life. They are likely to suffer adverse consequences for what they did when they were young – for example, by being turned down for a job they are applying for.

And this is not only true of cyber-bullying. Sending nude pictures to a girlfriend or boyfriend is not a good idea either. We should always think before we post. A good question to ask: "How would I feel if this were on TV tomorrow?" If you do not like that idea, then do not send or post the message

Summary

Smartphones and social media are wonderful ways to communicate. But they have downsides as well. There is the danger of overload and misunderstandings. Filter bubbles can determine how we feel. Cyber-bullying is an absolute no-no. And we need to think carefully before we put anything on record.

We need to be smart when using our smartphones and social media. That way we elevate our on-screen communication to a higher level.

5

Listen carefully and you can conquer the world

Introduction

When we think of communication, we often think of only one aspect: talking. But communication has two parts: talking and listening. Listening is often undervalued.

That is strange, because listening well is amongst the most important skills we can learn. Listening skills are more important than maths, English, history, and geography put together. A good listener can conquer the world. It is that simple.

At school, we often think of listening as being something a bit tiresome. "Listen to the teacher." Or, if you make a mistake, "You should listen more carefully!" But that's not what I mean here. What I'm talking about is the art of listening: listening to get the optimum outcome - teamwork between speaker and listener.

A good listener can avoid climbing higher and higher on the communication ladder. A conversation does not go wrong easily, and listening skills also help us reach our goals. Listening is an excellent skill. It's why we have two ears and one mouth – so we can listen twice as much as we speak!

Deep listening

We probably do not think about listening as a skill because it is so "normal" to listen. After all, we are listening all day. What can be so difficult or special about it?

Yes, we listen all day. Or rather, we hear. Are we really listening? It is a bit like the difference between looking and observing. We look around all day. Are we really observing what we see?

Fortunately, we do not listen to and observe absolutely everything we come across. If we did, we would go into overload meltdown in no time. We have filters that make sure that we don't take everything in.

Deep listening is extremely important. Interestingly, when we are listening deeply, it's not only our ears that we are using.

Listening with the eyes

It sounds strange, but this is how it works. Remember in Chapter Three we talked about non-verbal communication?

Gestures, facial expressions and body language are all elements of non-verbal communication. So it is not super strange that we can listen with our eyes.

In Chapter Three we saw that 58% of communication occurs without words. When we listen with our eyes, we pick up a lot of signals that we had not noticed before. This benefits us and the person we are having a conversation with.

The benefits of deep listening

There need to be at least two people for communication to take place: one or more listeners and a speaker – for example. us and a friend.

If we listen deeply, this has a beneficial effect on our friend.

- They feel respect from us;
- They feel we care about them;
- They feel understood.

This is quite something! We are actually making our friend feel good about themselves. But that's not all. The benefits also go the other way.

- The relationship with our friend gets even better;
- Our friend also wants to listen to us;
- We team up better;
- Our friend respects us more.

Deep listening is really valuable – but how can we learn it?

Passive and active listening

To become a good listener, we need to be aware that there are two roles in a conversation: listening and speaking. They are constantly changing positions.

When we are the listener, there are two ways we can listen: passive and active. Each way has its own elements. It is important to learn to recognise them.

Passive listening

We can recognise passive listening by the following elements:

- We are not really listening because we are distracted;
- We say "hmm" now and then, but we are not really participating;
- We do not look at the speaker;
- We give a nod now and then, but we do not know exactly why.

This is the type of listening we are engaged in when our mother asks us to put away our shoes while we are on our iPad. Or our father asks us how the exam went while we are on an app with a friend. Our focus is not really on the speaker.

We can get away with passive listening occasionally, but if we do this as we move higher up the communication ladder, we are in trouble. That is the moment when we have to start listening actively.

Active listening

When we listen actively, we put ourselves in the right frame of mind to absorb as much information as possible.

How?

- We make eye contact with the speaker;
- We are aware of non-verbal cues;
- We react at the right time;
- We do not interrupt;
- We ask questions.

If we can do this, we have got further than a lot of adults. Many adults have not learned how to do these things. Make the most of them!

How to use active listening

All this is nice to know, but you might be wondering what it has to do with you. That's easy. It's a matter of recognising what is happening and being able to use these skills. Let me explain how.

Recognise active listening in the other person

Imagine we have something important we want to discuss with a friend. We want our friend to listen actively so they can help us.

If we notice that our friend is listening passively, we can do two things:

1. Indicate that this is important;
2. Decide to have the conversation later.

It makes no sense to discuss something when our friend is not listening actively. It is a waste of time.

Recognising that our friend is only listening passively will also help us. We can ask amicably whether they have time for the conversation. If the answer is "no", we can ask when would suit them.

Applying active listening

Imagine that a friend has something important that they want to discuss with us. This is the moment that we can start exercising our active listening skills.

We look at our friend, which makes them feel our respect and appreciation. We pay attention to all non-verbal cues. What can we read in their facial expression? Sadness? Powerlessness? This is the first step in helping them.

We can give them feedback by nodding or saying something like: "Yes, I understand." But we do not interrupt, and we give them space to tell their story.

When there is a pause, we can ask questions to show that we care and are following what they say. This gives them a sense of being understood.

When we do this, we will notice that people open up to us more easily and more often. They tell us their concerns. This is not only beneficial for them, but also for us, because if everyone knows what is going on, we can work better together towards our goals. We are now able to help them – at school, in a team or in a group of friends.

The benefits of active listening

With active listening, we can conquer the world. This sounds dramatic, but it is true.

Active listening helps us to:

1. Save time;
2. Keep relationships healthy;
3. Reach our goals;
4. Increase our confidence.

Listening helps us save time

Having a chat is pleasant enough, and having a dialogue is great. But we do not want too many discussions and shouting-matches because they take up a lot of time and energy.

When we listen carefully, we know sooner whether having a discussion would be pointless – because now is not the right time to talk, or we are in the wrong place. Or because we realise that the person we were disagreeing with is right after all.

Listening keeps relationships healthy

To be happy and successful, we need good relationships. And teamwork in school or at work also requires good relationships.

When we consciously decide to listen, we become calmer in the course of a conversation. We are less concerned with our feelings and more with using our brains. This means there is less likelihood of having a shouting-match. And the other person will feel more valued when we listen.

Listening helps us reach our goals

When we get better at listening, it becomes easier to reach our goals. Want to be really good at soccer? Study to become a vet? A game developer? An actress? If we start by being a good listener, we will have the world at our fingertips. Because when we

are being good listeners, we understand the world better. We earn the respect of others and others wish us well. This helps us to reach our goals.

Listening increases our confidence

When we understand the world better, we reach more of our goals. When we reach our goals, we feel better about ourselves. We feel we can make a difference. We can do things, and our confidence grows.

When our confidence grows, our courage to do things grows with it. We stand more firmly in the world. A setback will not drag us down so easily. That way we go from strength to strength.

Summary

Listening is an especially important skill. Listening helps us to reach our goals and to keep our relationships healthy. We do not only listen with our ears, but also with our eyes. In active listening we use all our senses.

Through deep listening, we understand better what is going on. We get better at helping others, our confidence grows and it saves time. Success guaranteed!

6

Being a positive speaker

Introduction

During our lives, we will have to work in teams a lot – at school, at work and at home. We will not always agree with the other members of the team we are part of. And they may not agree with us. This is where intelligent communication comes in.

In this chapter we are going to look at how to be a positive speaker. Let us look at the communication ladder again.

The aim of communication

In Chapter Two we looked at the characteristics of each level of communication.

Let us go through them again:

A Chat

Just having a good time, sharing our stories.

A Dialogue

Sharing our opinions about a certain subject.

A Discussion

Things get a bit more intense. We try to convince each other of a particular viewpoint.

A Shouting-Match

Things get out of hand. We think we are right and the other person is wrong. We raise our voices. Other people do too. We talk over each other. We must put in a lot of energy to mend things afterwards, no matter whether we were right or wrong.

There is always a common goal

Why are we looking at these characteristics again? Because we have to be aware of the fact that there is always a common goal when we communicate. In a chat it is the sharing of stories; in a dialogue it is the sharing of our opinions.

What other goals could there be?

- Getting to the truth
- Finding the best solution
- Understanding something better
- Understanding each other better
- Adjusting our opinions
- Coming to a decision
- Accepting rules

It is really important to understand that communication is always about achieving a goal, and that there is always a common goal. It sounds impossible doesn't it? But whatever the subject of the discussion or argument, there always is this common goal.

For instance, you are having an argument with your brother over playing on the PlayStation or Xbox. The common goal is that you both want to play. So any time lost on arguing is costing you time – let's draw up a timetable and start playing.

Just having a good time is the goal of a chat.

Positive speakers reach their goals more often

Everybody has their own way of behaving in communication. The way we communicate is determined by our upbringing and by our education. What has worked best for us in the past also influences how we communicate.

We may be someone who always knows better. Or a calm person. Or we may be so enthusiastic that we always speak first. Or we wait for our turn. Or we sit back. It is all okay, if we are aware of what our behaviour is like.

And it is important to understand that there are certain ways of behaving that work better than others. There are positive ways of speaking – and there are negative ways. Let us first look at a positive speaker, because the positive speaker gets the most out of everything.

Focussed on solutions

A positive speaker thinks about the best outcome for all parties involved. If we want to make up after a shouting-match, we must keep that goal in mind when we speak. That way we do not waste time and we reach our goals sooner.

Take responsibility

Positive speakers do not pass the buck or walk away; they take responsibility. If they have said something nasty or were wrong about something, they admit it. Everyone respects someone who does this.

This way people have respect for us and we reach our goals more easily.

Daring to ask questions

Positive speakers are not afraid to ask for what they want. Whether they get it or not is not the issue. But if they do not ask, they will not get what they want.

Hey, Sam, the word is I'm not going to be playing in the match.

'Course you are Pete, you're the best keeper we have.

OK, great. I must have got it wrong somehow.

We should let people know what we need to reach our goals. That makes it easier to attain them.

Go to the horse's mouth

If we hear something we are not happy about, we should go to the source of the rumour. We should not talk with others about it first. We should not gossip. When we avoid gossip, we avoid irritation. We gain respect. People wish us well and we reach our goals sooner.

Negative speakers have a short shelf life

People with little confidence are often negative speakers. This is not a huge problem. Positive speaking can be learned. If we are aware of it, we can work on getting better at it.

What do negative speakers do?

Aggressive communication

Negative speakers turn communication into a competition. They want to be right. They lay blame. They raise their voices. They look stern and talk sternly.

Aggressive communication can work to reach our goals. But it works within a smaller group of people and only for a short time.

The older we get, the less this style of communication works. People get better at communicating as they get older and they do not put up with aggression.

Avoiding problems

Some negative speakers avoid problems by trying to be seen as nice all the time. When they do this, they underrate themselves and other people. They do not reach their goals. They give in to others and do not get what they want. That is not good for their confidence – and when their confidence disappears, even fewer goals are reached.

It is better to learn quickly how to do things differently.

Pretending to agree

This kind of negative speaker pretends to agree, but their behaviour shows otherwise. We notice this on a non-verbal level or simply by observing their actions.

It is possible to reach goals that way, but only in the short term. They say they agree, but they do the opposite. It doesn't take long for them to be rumbled. People soon lose respect for them. And when respect is lost, goals cannot be worked on as a team.

It is better to learn quickly not to do this.

What kind of speaker do we want to be?

Every day offers a new opportunity to decide what kind of speaker we want to be. We just have to decide what our attitude is.

Even if we are feeling a bit negative now, or we avoid robust discussion altogether, nothing has been lost. We have our whole lives in front of us to learn to communicate well. Today is a perfect day to decide to become a more positive speaker.

So there's no need to feel bad if we fail today. Nobody becomes a positive speaker in one day. Everybody needs time to learn how to communicate intelligently. Even the most gifted of us end up in a heated discussion now and then.

This is all part of the learning process.

Summary

Communication has common goals – sharing our stories; solving a problem. Positive speakers will reach these goals because they keep that goal in mind. They take responsibility, they have the courage to ask questions, and they go to the source. They do not gossip. Negative speakers reach fewer goals, and that makes them less confident. They become increasingly negative.

When we choose to be a positive speaker, we will find that people appreciate us, have respect for us and wish us well. In this way, being a positive speaker helps us to reach our goals.

7

The power of words

Introduction

People often think that words do no harm. They are only words. But this is not true. Words can cause more pain than a slap. The pain of a slap disappears after half an hour or so. Words, however, can stay in our heads for days. They influence how we feel.

Examples of the power of words

To show how powerful words are, here's a story and a question.

Imagine that tomorrow a virus is detected at our school. Nobody is allowed to leave the building. The school goes into lockdown.

Get the picture?

Doctors in white coats arrive to research the virus. At the end of the day they find a solution.

They have two possible medicines. Neither of them is perfect. We have to choose which one they will give us and our classmates.

Scenario 1

Medicine A: 200 of the 600 children will survive.

Medicine B: There is a 35% chance that everyone will survive, and a 65% chance that nobody will survive.

This is a difficult decision. We try to make up our minds. We take our time. And we continue reading only after we've made our choice.

Scenario 2

Now imagine the same situation. Again, the doctors develop two possible medicines. Again, they are not perfect. And again, we must choose.

Medicine A: It is certain that 400 of the 600 children will die.

Medicine B: there is a 35% chance that everybody will survive and a 65% that nobody will survive.

Again, this is difficult. Which to choose?

Most people choose A in the first scenario and B in the second. This is strange, because both cases give the same outcome. Read them again.

In both scenarios, B is the same. A is different. But they mean the same thing. What is different is that the order of ideas has been reversed: 200 of the 600 will survive, or 400 of the 600 will die. The difference lies in the words "die" or "survive". These words evoke strong positive or negative emotions.

This is a powerful example of how our decisions are influenced by the words we hear or read.

Positive or negative – the choices are in our hands

Every day we are in charge of the choices we make and the words we choose. We can choose to use positive words or negative words. Negative words often have the same effect as a virus.
Below are words that are often used. Notice the feelings they cause in us.

List 1

Yes, I can do that.
No problem.
I am pretty funny.
I look nice.
Together we can do it.
We've succeeded.
We are already halfway through it.
I am happy.
The sooner we start, the sooner we'll be finished.
It should not be too difficult.
Let's just give it a go.
I think we'll nail it.

How do you feel when reading these words? Take your time. Let us now look at the next list.

List 2

That is difficult.
It is a problem.
I am not sure if I will succeed.
I am stupid.
I am ugly.
We cannot do it.
It's gone wrong.
We are only halfway through.
Will it really be all right?
I am unhappy.
We do not know if we can finish it.
It will be tricky.
Maybe we should not do it.
I think it will go wrong.

How do you feel when you read this list? You have probably noticed that positive language makes you happier. The negative words drain your energy. Can you see how powerful words on paper are? They are even more powerful when you say them out loud.

'Super Peter' outfit

'Sad Sam' outfit

Our words influence how people perceive us

The words we use determine how we feel. But that is not the whole story. The words we use also influence how we are perceived by the people we live with.

Do we mainly use positive words or negative words? For most of us the answer is somewhere in the middle.

It is helpful to realise that our words make a difference – that they leave a positive or a negative impression. If we often use negative words often, we are likely to notice that others start to react to us in a negative way.

How do we feel when we look at the picture above? Daisy is dreading the test coming up. Lola is more optimistic and wants to start studying. Daisy uses a lot of negative words ("It is a lot of work... it's really hard."). Lola uses positive words ("We can do it... Let's get started!").

Daisy may not mean to come across as negative, but that's the way she is perceived by Lola. Lola may end up thinking, "I'd prefer to work on this by myself."

Daisy now has an even bigger problem. She must work alone and has lost a friend. Daisy is also talking herself down, because our words not only influence the people around us – they influence us as well.

We listen to ourselves all day (subconsciously)

Maybe even more important than the effects of our words on other people are the effects that our words have on ourselves. We hear ourselves when we talk. If what we hear is mainly negative, we will build a negative self-image. This is not really what we want.

Not only do we hear ourselves when we talk; we also think in words. We communicate mostly with ourselves. The way we think has a huge influence on the way we feel – and the way we feel influences our actions.

Our actions influence other people. Actions determine how others see us and what others say and do. Like in the picture below.

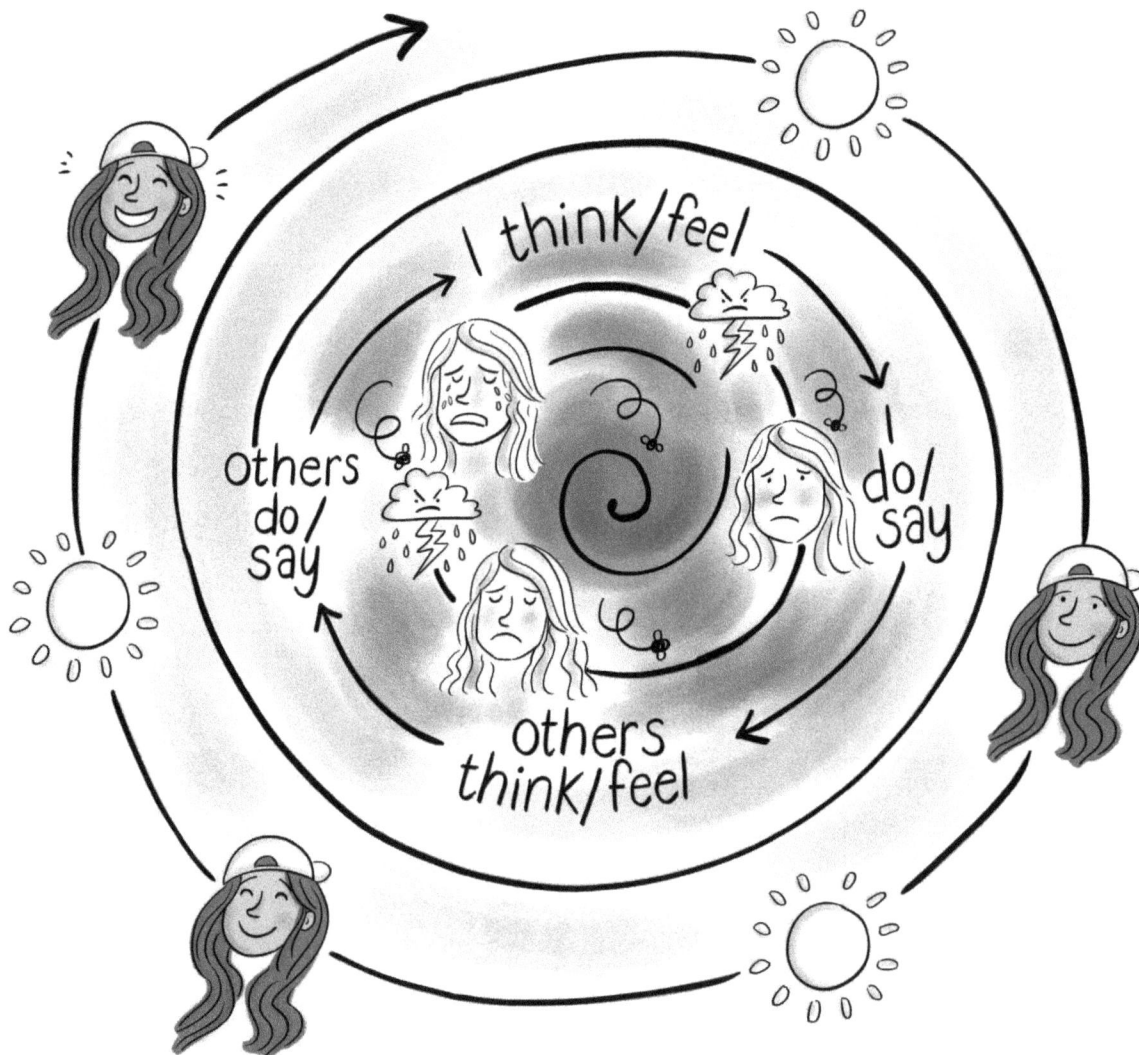

The most important part here is the outer spiral. When we use positive language, our actions are also more positive. Other people see us as more positive. They speak and behave more positively towards us. We start to feel better. The spiral goes upwards.

The other possibility is that we use mainly negative language. This too influences the people around us. How they see us and how they react to us. We may end up in the inner spiral. This is a downward spiral. Not nice to be in at all.

Using the right words makes things go more smoothly

We communicate because we want to reach a certain goal. Look at the communication ladder again and the goals that go with each step:

Level	Goal
A chat	Sharing our stories
A dialogue	Sharing our opinions
A discussion	Trying to convince others
A shouting-match	Trying to get our way at all costs

The words we use will determine whether we reach our goal or not. If we use negative language, it will be more difficult to reach our goals. When we use positive words, we will reach our goals faster.

Words do not only influence how we and others feel and act. They also influence whether we ourselves reach our goals. Try to choose to be positive most of the time.

A powerful presence

Positive language makes everyone grow. Let us think about a time we received a compliment. Did it make us feel good? Of course it did!

All people, young and old, rich and poor, need positivity in their lives. Not necessarily in the form of compliments. Just being there, having someone's back, means a lot. Listening. Saying a few positive words. Reminding them of what they are good at – just as Daisy does with Lola in the drawing.

People view us differently when we switch to using positive language. It gives us a powerful presence, and people like that.

Summary

Words are extremely powerful. They influence the world around us and how we see ourselves. It is our choice whether we want to use positive or negative words. Negative words often cause negative actions, by us and by others. Positive words result in positive actions.

8

People communicate differently

Introduction

Over the course of our lives, we will communicate with a variety of people. Communication will be easier with some of them than with others. People differ in looks. They also differ in communication styles. A good example is what you find at school – students vary in looks and in the way they communicate.

Students come in all shapes and sizes

Students come in a lot of varieties. Highly gifted people may have less difficulty in learning – but they may have social difficulties. Communicating with them can be a different experience. Differently abled kids communicate differently too. Kids with a hearing disability communicate differently. Those who are vision-impaired communicate differently. We need to adapt our communication styles in order to reach our goals.

Gestures mean different things in different cultures

Gestures are different in different cultures. In many countries in the West (though not all), when we give a "thumbs up" we mean that we approve, or that we are satisfied. In Japan, however, sticking up a thumb means "men"(and sticking up a pinky means "women"). In the West, we point at our chests to indicate "me". Japanese people point at their noses. In the Middle East it is better to avoid using this gesture altogether. It means that we are telling the person we don't like what they are saying.

First language, second language....

For many Australian Aborigine and Torres Strait Islanders, English is not their first language. Some speak several languages. English may be their third, fourth or even fifth language. Some may speak a dialect such as Kriol, Aboriginal English or Torres Strait Creole. Cultural awareness is needed for communicating intelligently.

The use of silence

In some Aboriginal and Torres Strait Islander cultures, long periods of silence in a conversation are the norm and are valued. Silences are used for listening and to show respect or agreement. In the West we are not used to long silences. We may experience them as awkward

Being on time

In the West, we think of being on time as important. We need to meet deadlines, we schedule. In Aboriginal and Torres Strait Islander cultures, however, more value is placed on family responsibilities and community relationships. Rushing is seen as unhealthy.

Be aware of stereotypes

Although the differences between cultures are entertaining and interesting, it is important that we do not stereotype. For many Indigenous people, English is now the first language. Being aware of stereotypes and being aware of differences becomes a balancing act that leads to intelligent and considerate communication.

Directness and reserve

American, German and Dutch people can be very direct. This can feel terribly rude to someone from India, the UK or Australia. English and Asian people tend to be more reserved.

Always try to remember that people are communicating in the way they were taught by their culture. Most of the time they do not mean to appear blunt and are not timid at all. They are just being true to their upbringing in communicating.

The communication ladder

From a young age onwards, we meet people from different backgrounds, from different cultures, and of different abilities. The younger we start, the better we will be at communicating intelligently with everybody we meet. The communication ladder is a useful tool to guide us to communicate well with everyone we meet.

A large part of intelligent communication is about understanding the other person. Communicating with people from different backgrounds, cultures and abilities gives us the ability to develop our Social- Emotional Skills.

A shouting-match

A discussion

A dialogue

A chat

Summary

During our lifetimes, we communicate with a wide variety of people from different backgrounds, abilities and cultures. This can be challenging, but it is an opportunity to develop our Social-Emotional Skills. When we learn to communicate intelligently, with a wide variety of people, we get better at reaching our goals.

9

Baking good communication

Introduction

When we bake a cake, we need the right ingredients. Eggs, butter, flour, sugar, and some lemon rind. Getting hungry yet?

The same counts for communication. We need the right ingredients to make it work. Having a chat may be easy, but to have a good dialogue we need the right ingredients.

The basic ingredients of communication are:

- A point of view
- An argument
- A counterargument

In this chapter we will look at these closely one by one, so that we learn to use them well.

A point of view

Our point of view is simply our opinion about something or someone.

For example:

- Bananas taste better than apples
- Tesla makes the best cars
- Geography is a boring subject
- Chimps are funnier than gorillas

Observe how points of view work in a conversation between two girlfriends.

Daisy and Lola have known each other forever. They often get together. But Lola is often late. Daisy wants to discuss this with Lola. Daisy's point of view is: 'My friend Lola is often late'. The way she puts it to Lola is a little more friendly.

Daisy:
"I've noticed you're a bit later than the time we settled on. That's a pity, because I was looking forward to seeing you and I had to wait."

Now two things can happen. Lola agrees or she does not agree.

If she agrees she will say something like:

Lola:
"I know, I often lose track of time. I will try to get better at being punctual."

If she does not agree, she may say:

Lola:
"I don't know what you're talking about. I always turn up, don't I?"

If the latter occurs, Daisy must convince Lola that she, Daisy, is right. She will use arguments to do so.

Argument

The argument is the reason why you have your point of view. There can be more than one argument for your point of view.

For example:

Daisy:
"I've noticed you're a bit later than the time we agreed. That's a pity, because I was looking forward to seeing you and I had to wait."
Lola:
"I do not know what you are talking about. I always turn up, don't I?"
Daisy:
"Well... take last Friday. We'd said 4pm and you turned up at 5."

Daisy has now used an argument to build her case and prove she is right.

Again, two things can happen. The first possibility is easy. Lola says: "Sorry, I'll be more considerate next time." The air has been cleared and their relationship is steady. Daisy feels good that she has reached her goal.

The second possibility is trickier. We start from the beginning:

Daisy:
"I've noticed you're a bit later than the time we agreed. That's a pity, because I was looking forward to seeing you and I had to wait."
Lola:
"I don't know what you're talking about. I always turn up, don't I?"
Daisy:
"Well... take last Friday. We'd said 4pm and you turned up at 5."
Lola:
"No, Daisy, we said 5pm last Friday."

Lola has her own argument that is the opposite of Daisy's argument

Counter-argument

A response that tries to show our argument is wrong.

The conversation continues as follows:

Daisy:
"I've noticed you're a bit later than the time we agreed. That's a pity, because I was looking forward to seeing you and I had to wait."
Lola:
"I don't know what you're talking about. I always turn up, don't I?"
Daisy:
"Well...take last Friday. We'd said 4pm and you turned up at 5."
Lola:
"No, Daisy, we said 5pm last Friday."
Daisy:
"Really?"
Lola:
"Yes, really. Otherwise I would have come at 4pm, silly."

Daisy:
"How come I thought we said 4pm?"
Lola:
"I don't know. Here, look at this text. It says 5pm."

Lola has not only given her counterargument; she has also given evidence. That is pretty powerful.

Apparently, Daisy made a mistake. When you make a mistake, it is best to admit it. Daisy says: "Okay, sorry I brought it up." And everything is okay, and both feel strong. Daisy feels good because she had the courage to bring it up. Lola feels good because she changed Daisy's point of view.

The ingredients were right. The communication went well.

Arguments: facts or opinions?

One reason why communication goes wrong is when arguments are based on opinions instead of facts. A fact is something that we can prove. If we cannot prove our argument, it is an opinion. There is nothing wrong with opinions, but it is important to recognise the difference.

Example: In a conversation we state that fruit cake is better than cheesecake.

According to us that is a fact. But it is, in fact, our opinion. Why? There is no proof that fruit cake is better than cheesecake. There will be plenty of people stating the opposite. These people are also stating their opinion.

When we present our opinion as fact, others get irritated. They know or feel it is merely an opinion. When we maintain it is a fact, the conversation gets tricky.

The chances are that we will climb higher on the communication ladder, to the level of a discussion or even a shouting-match.

That is why it is better to use arguments that are made up of facts.

Take the fruit cake example. Imagine research has been done amongst 10.000 people. 80% of those people say that fruit cake is better than cheesecake. We will then be able to say: "Most people like fruit cake better."

That is a fact.

How to distinguish the different flavours?

The examples above are simple. The reality is, of course, more complex. There are often more than two points of view – and more arguments and counterarguments. Often things heat up to a discussion or even a shouting-match. And when it gets that way it is difficult to see what is going on.

People who are good at analysing what is going on in such a situation are extremely useful, in their family, amongst friends and in a team. They are the glue between people.

We can learn how to recognise the different ingredients. It is easiest when we are not part of the conversation, but an observer. We can try it when we are watching a series on TV.

1. Try to figure out what a person's point of view is
2. Listen for arguments
3. Are they facts or opinions?
4. Listen for counterarguments

It is useful to recognise signal words:

Point of view	Argument	Counterargument
I think….	Because…	That's not true, because….
If you ask me…	Firstly…	I don't agree, because….
It is a fact that…	Secondly….	No, because…
My opinion is…	What's more…	That's not correct, because…

It is useful if we are able to recognise point of view, argument and counterargument. Only when we recognise them will we be able to handle them one by one. This way, we can come closer to our goals.

Summary

Intelligent communication has three important ingredients: point of view, argument, and counterargument. When we learn to recognise them, we communicate better. Signal words can be a big help. We should make sure we use facts, not opinions to build our argument.

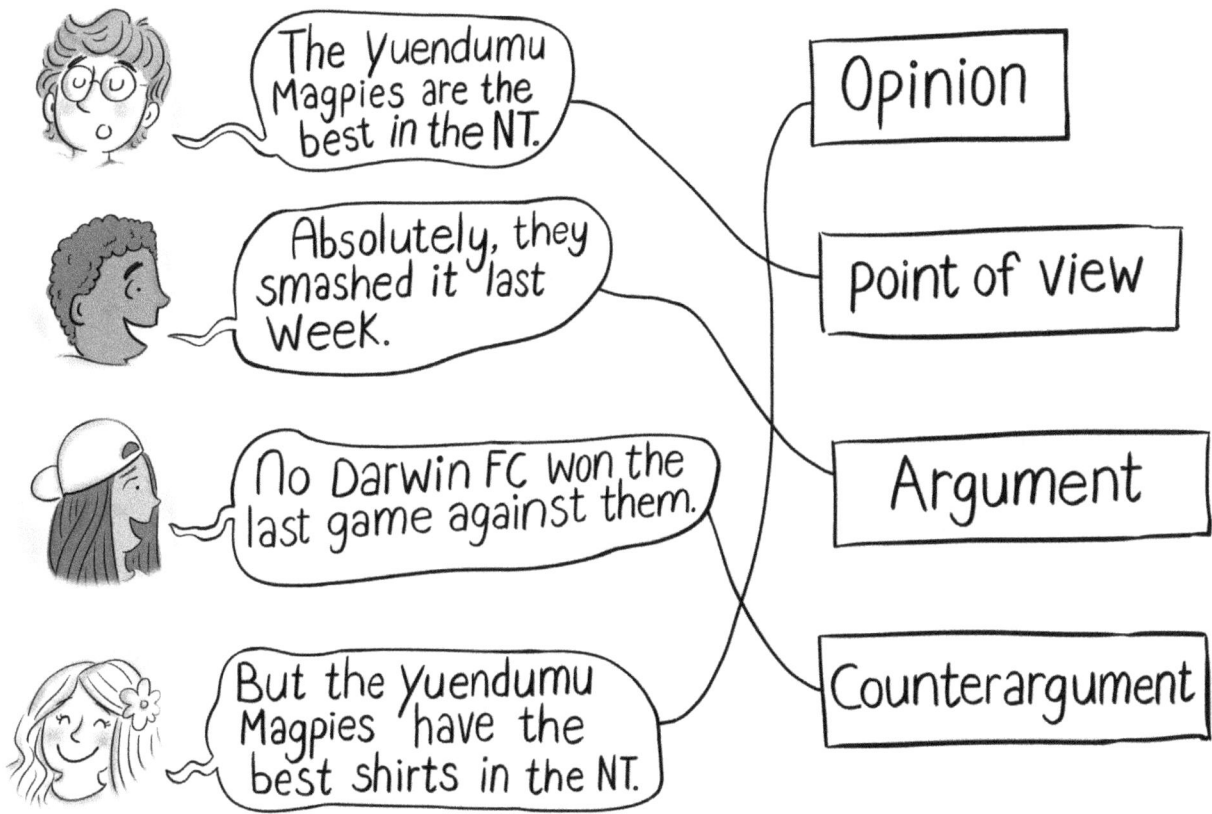

The Yuendumu Magpies are the best *in the* NT.

Absolutely, they smashed it last week.

No Darwin FC won the last game against them.

But the Yuendumu Magpies have the best shirts in the NT.

Opinion

Point of view

Argument

Counterargument

10

Silence is our friend

Introduction

Silence forms a part of every conversation, and it can be a powerful tool. Silence can be stressful, or it can be relaxing. In some cultures, silence is valued highly; in others it is seen as awkward.

What we often do not realise is that silence is important.

The silence between words

IfItalkedtoyoulikethisyouwouldnotgetmuch of what I was saying, would you?

The silences between our words have a meaning. When these silences are long, it means we are thinking about what we are saying, or that we are relaxed, or both. When we rattle on, it can mean that we are not giving much thought to what we are saying, or that we are enthusiastic, nervous, or angry.

The higher we climb on the communication ladder, the less silence there is between words. During a shouting-match, words tumble over one another.

Silence in art

Silence in music is just as important as the notes we play or hear. Think of it – silence is part of the rhythm and harmony of music. Without silence between the notes, there would not be a rhythm or melody at all – just a cacophony of noise. And think about the background of a painting or drawing – that is a kind of silence too. Nothing happens there, but it is important. Space holds the

In Western cultures we connect the dots (stars) and see the shape of an animal or thing. In some other cultures it is the the dark shape between the stars that is more important: this is what is observed and described as the animal or thing.

objects that are depicted. In a black-and-white drawing, the white is as important as the black.

Silence helps us understand

When we communicate, we should not be afraid of silence. Silence is our friend. When we are silent, we are listening, and when we do that we often learn something. If we find ourselves high up on the communication ladder and then fall silent, we give ourselves room to think and to come to our senses. We also give room to the people we are communicating with. Silence may also give them insights on how to resolve the issue at hand.

Awkward silences

Silence causes the people we talk with to feel good. They feel heard. Their words are taken seriously. Long silences are great tools of intelligent communication. When asked a challenging question, instead of answering, we pause and think deeply about the answer. Make no mistake, this is no short pause. We may go silent for five, ten, or even fifteen seconds before answering.

If we are not used to doing this, it will feel awkward at first. However, it leads to better communication and helps us reach our goals.

Using silence to come back down

Silence helps us to give better, more thoughtful answers. It helps us to get to the root of a problem; it leads us to better understanding. It brings us down the communication ladder. If our discussion gets too heated and could escalate to a shouting-match, we can use silence to come back down to the dialogue level.

Use silence before answering a question

When answering a challenging question, we may be tempted just to say the first thing that comes into our heads, even if does not make much sense. Or we may say what we think the other person wants to hear, instead of what we honestly believe. Is that what we really want?

Or do we prefer to take a few seconds' pause, to think things through, and then to respond in a way we can be proud of later? Using silence to our advantage before answering is a wise move.

Emotional intelligence and silence

Emotional intelligence is the ability to manage emotions. When it comes to calm thinking, we use a part of our brain known as the Prefrontal Cortex. When we feel attacked or under pressure, we engage a part called the Amygdala, which can cause an "emotional hijack." That is not always a bad thing, as our emotions can help us get out of difficult situations. It becomes a problem when we are not aware of it and we say or do things that we later regret. Silence can calm an Amygdala reaction.

Is that you speaking, or just your Amygdala?

The advantages of silence

Silence buys us time to think; puts us in the drivers' seat; shows respect; keeps us calm; increases our confidence; produces better answers; makes us say what we mean and mean what we say; and makes emotions work for us, instead of against us. After a while an awkward silence won't feel so awkward any more – rather, it becomes a handy tool in our communication toolbox.

Summary

The silences between our words have meaning. Silence is the background for sound. Silence is our friend. Silence builds emotional intelligence. It puts us in the driver's seat and gives us control over a conversation. It helps us to descend the communication ladder. Even awkward silences can be turned into a useful tool.

11

Formulate logically

Introduction

To communicate our points of view, we should use arguments and counter-arguments as intelligently as possible, along with clear language.

To reach our goals it is important that we use the right words and ideas in the right order. This is called "formulating logically".

Formulating Logically: Ordering our words, sentences and ideas so that the chance of reaching our goals is maximised.

Before we continue with formulating logically, let's look at different kinds of people.

Three kinds of people

In a simplified world there are three kinds of people:

1. People who think before they speak;
2. People who think while they speak;
3. People who speak before they think.

Which of the three are we? We would all like to say we belong to Group 1. We like to see ourselves as being calm, collected, balanced, mindful, and logical.

But it is not that simple. We are different people in different situations. In one we are calm and think before we speak; in another we react impulsively, excitedly, without thinking. It depends on how tired we are, whether we are under pressure, and on our character.

But if we want to reach our goals, we had better belong to Group 1. When we think before we speak it is much easier to formulate logically.

The four steps of formulating logically

So, formulating logically is important. But how do we go about it? To learn this we need some structures in place. Such as:

1. Think before we speak
2. Important things first
3. Only one thing at a time
4. Short clear sentences

Think before we speak

People often just say things without thinking about them. Whatever comes up in their mind, they say it. This is no problem when we are having a chat. But it becomes problematic if we want to have a dialogue or discussion. It is important that we think carefully before we speak.

Let us ask ourselves:

- Is what I am going to say related to what we are talking about?

- Is my point of view / opinion helpful for resolving the issue?

If we can say "yes" to both these questions, we can start speaking.

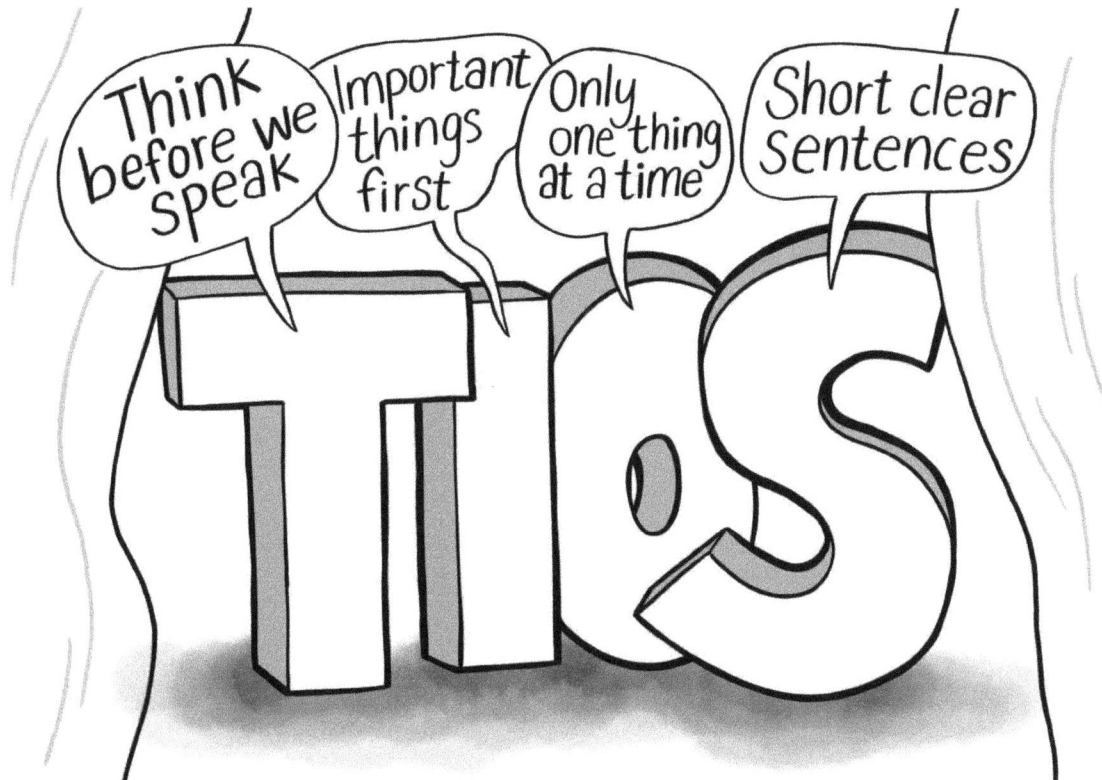

Let us look at Peter as an example:

Situation	Peter sits in class, thinking...
Summers are getting hotter and hotter. It is another scorching hot summer's day. Year 8 students are discussing with their teacher whether it would be beneficial to move onto a summer timetable for the rest of the summer, because it is still relatively cool in the early mornings. This would mean starting earlier and finishing earlier.	I have an opinion about this. I think I can help us reach our goal here. Great! That is two yesses. Let's move on.

Important things first

In a chat it does not really matter where we begin. But we should not be that random when in a dialogue or discussion. Do we have more than one idea in mind? We should begin with the most important one.

Begin with our point of view. Our point of view is our opinion. Or what we stand for. What goal do we want to reach in the conversation? Back to Peter:

Situation	Peter says...
In class, people are talking about the hot weather.	"Miss, I think we should implement a summer timetable for the rest of the summer." Bang! Peter has given his opinion in one short, clear sentence.

One thing at a time

In a chat we can jump from one subject to another. The conversation goes all over the place. No problem. But in a dialogue or a discussion, it is better to say one thing at a time.

In our Peter example, Peter probably has several reasons (arguments) why he thinks it is better to move to a summer timetable. He lists them in his head – first his point of view, then his arguments.

Situation	Peter says...
The teacher asks: Why do you think we should switch to a summer roster?	It will be over 40 degrees in the coming weeks, and our school's air-conditioning system is not the best.

Use short sentences

Short sentences. Full stops and pauses. They are all important in getting our point across. Especially when we have more than one argument.

Peter may have even more than two reasons. Below he lists them in a logical way:

Situation	Peter says...
The teacher asks: Why do you think we should switch to a summer roster?	"There are a couple of reasons. Firstly, it will be over 40 degrees in the coming weeks. Secondly, our school's air-conditioning system is not the best. Thirdly, studying in the heat is less effective. Fourthly, the summer holidays are almost here." Bang! Peter has given four reasons (arguments) why the summer timetable should be implemented. They are nicely listed. His argument is clear.

This way we communicate our point of view and our arguments in a logical way. We have a clear structure.

Imagine that Sam adds to Peter's argument: "And we have already finished the whole curriculum anyway."

This can be listed with Peter's argument to make it even stronger. Peter now has five arguments why they should implement the summer timetable. It is almost certain that a summer timetable will be implemented, don't you think?

When we communicate this way, we are clear and most likely to reach our goals.

Easy, isn't it?

There are several pitfalls, though.

Four pitfalls that get in the way of logical communication

Let us also look at how not to do it. We may recognise some of the examples in ourselves. Not a problem! We have more than enough time to improve.

Talking too much

Some people cannot stop talking. They do not seem to be aware that a conversation should have two people in it. But when we talk, we do not learn anything. When we talk and do not listen, we have no way of checking whether our communication is working. We need to pause once in a while and let other people do the talking. That way we learn what their opinions are – and people do not get irritated with us.

Straying off-topic

Some people stray off-topic. They wander a long way off the subject at hand.

Our brains are good at making connections. One thing reminds us of another thing… but if we do not mentally check ourselves, the next thing we find ourselves doing is talking about that other subject.

This is confusing for listeners. What were we talking about? What was our goal? What are our points of view? If we stray off-topic, things become unclear and we are unlikely to reach our goals.

Daisy's Aunt Rosa has just entered the room. She begins to talk: "I took the bus and said to the driver, 'oh, isn't the weather nice!' But he doesn't say a word. It was like talking to a brick wall or your uncle Phil. But well, in Phil's case it may be because of his backache. We were at the hospital for his back, you know, and the doctor was so nice! I said to him, 'You can keep Phil for a week if you like, while we go out and enjoy ourselves!' But the doc didn't even smile. No-one has a sense of humour nowadays, do they? Not like they used to. I remember during the war...."

Selling ourselves short

Some people never get to the point. They do not want to hurt anyone's feelings, or are too shy to give their opinion. They talk but they do not say much. This is a pity.

If you want to reach your goal you have to be clear about your intentions. Be direct. In a polite way of course but be clear about what you want to achieve.

Sam hears a rumour that a group of boys will be going into town that afternoon. He says: "Hey, cool, what time are you guys going? Or maybe you prefer it just to be the four of you. You think I could..... I mean, if you guys are going by bicycle, I could... you've got to be honest about it though.... I don't mind if...."

It would be better for Sam just to say: "Hey, can I join you guys?"

Too many details

Some people throw in everything they have and more when it comes to making their point. This can muddy the waters. If we add too much detail, our listeners have to listen hard for our main point – it is drowning in a soup of information.

Of course details are important in a discussion. But not at the beginning. And certainly not too many. If we want to achieve something, we have to express it – to be clear about our goals. This is good communication.

How do we react?

We know now what not to do. But how do we go about dealing with people who talk too much, drift off-topic, or beat around the bush?

Just ask them to get to the point. Wait for a good moment to interrupt the stream of words, then ask in a friendly voice: "Sorry, I don't understand your point. Can you be clearer? Can you be more precise?"

It is not weird to do this, and the discussion moves more on-topic.

What else can we do to communicate logically?

If we master and apply the four elements of formulating logically, we are good. If we add the following four points, we are a communication champion.

1. Being honest
2. Being direct
3. Being positive
4. Being clear

Together they form a great communication skill-set.

Being honest

Being honest is important. It is appreciated in every situation. If we have been wrong about something, it is important to admit it. That way we will reach our goals faster.

"I did not do my homework, Miss. My weekend was too busy", instead of:

"I had just finished it. Then my brother spilled his milk all over it. It was too late to start again."

Being direct (but not blunt)

If we are direct, we are clear. Being direct is different from being blunt. Being direct is telling the truth based on the facts. It does not include being hurtful.

For example: "That was not your best work", instead of: "That's terrible."

Being positive

Build the other person up instead of knocking them down. Give suggestions on how to do it better. Critiquing something is okay, but not if we have no idea how to do it better.

For example:

"That wasn't your best presentation. Usually you are calm. But you seemed to be nervous. Was it because you forgot your notes?"

Being clear

When we have landed in a discussion, it is important to be clear. Certain words and phrases can cause confusion.

For example:

- Maybe I can do better.
- I'm going to try to do better.
- I'll see if I can do it tomorrow.
- I could try to do it this week.

These sentences are unclear. It is not clear whether we are going to it or not. This is not good for the other person. Neither is it good for us. People like clarity. People who are clear earn respect. By being clear, we show others our strength.

But again, it is not only the words that count. If we say: "I will do it tomorrow" and we do not do it tomorrow, we have the same problem tomorrow as we have today.

Summary

Formulating communication logically is about delivering our point loudly and clearly. We had better think before we speak. We should start with the most important thing. Convey one thing at a time and use short sentences. That way we get our point across.

Avoid pitfalls like talking too much, beating around the bush and swerving off-topic. They weaken our communication. Communication champions are honest, direct, positive, and clear.

12

Beware of assumptions

Introduction

As we climb higher on the communication ladder, communication becomes more and more tricky. When we are having a discussion, it is easy to end up in a shouting-match. Communication is about being aware.

In the coming three chapters, we look at three important pitfalls to be aware of. In this chapter we discuss assumptions.

What is an assumption?

An assumption is something that is accepted as true without question or proof. Our brain just tells us it is true. But sometimes our brain is wrong. This can cause huge misunderstandings.

Assumptions can easily lead to discussions or dialogues ending up as shouting-matches. In the US there is a saying: "Assumptions are the mother of all divorces." This gives us an idea of how huge the problem is.

Situation	Daisy's assumption	Lola's disappointment
A group of girls is walking away from the school yard. Lola is talking with one of them, so she follows the group.	Daisy sees Lola walk away with the group. Daisy thinks Lola prefers the group to her. She walks home alone, disappointed.	Lola turns around and wants to walk towards Daisy. They had a deal to do their homework together. But Daisy is nowhere to be seen. Lola feels disappointed.

That day the relationship between Daisy and Lola is not great. This could have been avoided if Daisy had not assumed anything.

Humour is often based on assumptions. Strange situations can easily arise out of assumptions. For example:

In a game based on trust, one person stands blindfolded in a room, while behind them people stand ready to catch them when they let themselves fall.

The leader of the game says to the blindfolded person: "Are you ready? Fall!"

The blindfolded person falls forwards instead of backwards. There is no one to catch them. All the catchers are standing behind them, because everyone assumes the blindfolded person will fall backwards. Instead of trust, the blindfolded person ends up with a bump on their forehead.

How do assumptions arise?

Our brains are sophisticated and fast. When we have experienced something, the information is stored for later use. The result is that we have a giant database in our heads containing all kinds of important information.

For example: we see an orange glow and feel heat. We assume this means there is a fire. Our brain signals: keep away! This signal is useful. But the same database can also cause problems.

When the brain assumes something that is not in fact true, all kinds of problems can arise.

There are all sorts of situations that lead to assumptions. Let's look at a few.

Assumptions based on tone of voice or body language

Some assumptions arise not from what we say, but how we say it. Remember, only 7% of communication is rooted in words. 35% comes from tone of voice and 58% from body language.

Example: We are talking with a friend at the same time as we are looking into the light. Because of the light we are screwing up our eyes slightly, but this makes our expression stern and serious. Our friend assumes we are angry and responds with an angry reaction themselves.

Or we say something in a tone that indicates the opposite of what our words mean. Our point comes across much more negatively than we intended as a result of our non-verbal communication.

Assumptions based on behaviour

Everyone must have experienced this. We see people interacting and think it is about us. For example, when there is laughing in class, and someone looks at us, we assume they are laughing at us. Or when our friend does not react to something we say immediately, we think they do not like us. When this happens, we react based on an assumption. This can cause trouble and miscommunication.

Assumptions based on badly formulated communication

A discussion can sometimes get heated. When our heart rate goes up and the tension builds, it is increasingly difficult to communicate intelligently. We may say something we did not mean. But people cannot look into our heads. They assume that we meant what we said. This can cause the discussion to heat up and become a shouting-match.

Assumptions based on written communication

We use Snapchat, Instagram and WhatsApp to communicate every day. But because we see only a fraction of the communication, it can easily go wrong. We have no tone of voice or non-verbal cues to guide us.

Assumptions from not listening well

When tension arises in a discussion, people listen less carefully. This is understandable but it causes problems. Because even though they haven't listened well, they assume that they have heard correctly, and usually that what they have heard is negative. This causes more tension and even shouting-matches.

Assumptions based on upbringing and culture

Everything we have experienced determines what our assumptions are.

Until the 15th century it was assumed that the earth was flat, and that people would fall off if they ventured too far out to sea.

If we grow up in a neighbourhood full of expensive cars, we assume this is the norm. Our accumulated experiences determine how we communicate. There are too many assumptions to list. Fortunately, there is a solution.

Use: Do you mean that...?

There is an easy way to handle assumptions. Ask: "Do you mean that...?" There are two situations in which we need to think about using "Do you mean that...?"

1. When we listen

Imagine someone says something that makes us furious. We want to react by saying something even more outrageous.

Take a deep breath and repeat what the other person just said. Start with: "Do you mean that....?" And then repeat what you think you heard.

2. When we speak

This also works when we are asked the question: "Do you mean that....?"

It forces us to think. Was that what we said? Was that what we meant? If not, we can correct it.

These are two simple rules that will help us avoid assumptions. They make sure we have understood something correctly and are not making assumptions. By following these we will react to facts rather than assumptions.

Situation	Step	Action
Something someone says makes us angry	1	Take a deep breath
	2	"Do you mean that….?"
	3	Listen to the answer.
Someone uses "Do you mean that…?" on us	1	Take a deep breath
	2	Listen to "Do you mean that…?"
	3	Is that what you said and meant to say?
	4	Adjust if necessary.

Why does "Do you mean that…?" work?

When we use "Do you mean that…?", we are making sure we have understood. That way we do not react to things that aren't really there.

By using "Do you mean that…?"

1. We check whether we have understood what the other person said or did;

2. We give the other person a chance to correct themselves;

3. We create some space in the conversation. We are both forced to think;

4. We show we are not afraid to clarify. People respect that.

Vary "Do you mean that...?"

We do not have to say it in the same way each time we use it. There are other ways of saying the same thing:

- Do I understand you right, that....?
- I understand you are saying that....
- You mean....
- In other words,....
- You want to say that...
- Are you trying to say that...?
- So, you mean...
- Do you mean it when you say....?
- What I'm hearing is.... Is that right?

Tip: remain calm while asking

Every person is different. For some it is easy to remain calm, for others it is more difficult. Some people are quicker to make assumptions than others. If one of the two remains calm, trouble can be prevented. Goals are reached sooner, and time and energy are saved.

We should be calm when we say: "Do you mean that...?" Do not yell it. If we ask it in a calm way, it signals to the other person that we are interested in their opinion. The other person will then take time to check and correct themselves.

We will notice that assumptions are hard to avoid. But if we practise, it gets easier. After practising for a while, we get used to avoiding assumptions.

Assumptions and prejudices are similar

One kind of assumption is prejudice. People have a lot of these. They are hard to get rid of and can cause a lot of problems.

The word is self-explanatory: 'pre' means 'before', and 'judices' means 'judgements'. - that is, to judge something before you have the facts – when an opinion is so strong that it is difficult to look at the facts. We simply presume something to be the case. Prejudices are deadly because they can kill any dialogue or discussion.

Examples:

- Netball is just for girls
- If you are not good at school, you will get nowhere
- Chess is boring
- Soccer is not for girls
- Ballet is not for boys

We encounter hundreds of these assumptions in our daily lives. They are all nonsense. Some are harmless, but others cause wars.

If we communicate intelligently, we take care to use facts while in discussion or dialogue. If we agree about the facts, we can have a robust and healthy discussion.

Try to enter a discussion neutrally. That way we form an opinion based on the facts and not based on assumptions.

Summary

An important pitfall in communication is making assumptions. An assumption leads to choices that are not based on facts. These choices are often wrong. This leads to difficult situations. We can avoid these by using "Do you mean that…?" This can clarify a lot of things.

This way we communicate intelligently, which helps us reach our goals. We gain good friends and that makes us happy.

13

Avoid swerving off-topic

Introduction

In the previous chapter we discussed the first pitfall in communication: assumptions. In this chapter we look at swerving off-topic. Swerving transforms a discussion into a dense forest where nothing makes sense.

What is swerving?

Let's first have a look what we mean by swerving. Swerving is when you jump from one topic to another in a discussion, without resolving the first one.

For example: one day we tell a friend that we did not appreciate it that she was talking about us behind our back. We said that it made us sad. We also said that good friends do not talk about each other behind the other's back.

Instead of responding to what we said, our friend said: "But you went into town with Annabel last week and I didn't like that."

This is swerving. We were addressing talking behind someone's back. Our friend starts an entire new and unrelated topic. When this happens, alarm bells should start ringing! Because if we are not careful, we will be swept away in the new argument. We are likely to say what we, in turn, did not like about our friend. Before we know it, we have ended up having a serious shouting-match.

Even when we are the one speaking, we need to pay attention. It is easy to fall into this trap ourselves. We want to illustrate something and add another subject. And before we know it, we cannot see the forest for the trees!

The causes of swerving off-topic

There are two causes of swerving:

1. Our super-fast brains

Our brains make connections between the information they store. When someone tells a story about their trip to Tasmania, the other person makes connections relating to their own experiences.

This happens between Peter and Sam as follows:

Sam says	Peter thinks
I went to Tasmania in the holidays.	I've been there. Cold country. I went to Hobart and played soccer with some boys.
We went camping on Bruny Island.	Don't know Bruny, but Hobart was nice. It has a harbour and you can see Mount Wellington from there.
We went on long bush walks and cooked dinner over a fire.	Cooking over a fire... I did that when I was camping with the scouts. We ate hot marshmallows. They were delicious!

Sam has said three sentences and Peter's brain has made a lot of connections. But Sam cannot look into Peter's head.

Do you think the conversation about camping on Bruny Island will last? Probably not. That is not a problem if we are just having a chat. But if we are in dialogue or discussion or in a shouting-match, it's better not to swerve off-topic.

2. Unresolved emotions

The stronger the emotion, the stronger the memory. If we have unresolved emotions, our memory of them will be vivid. Here too, the brain makes connections while the other person talks.

For example, here is a conversation between Daisy and Lola. Lola has a couple of unresolved emotions:

Lola says	Daisy thinks
Daisy, shall we go to the show next weekend?	Yes great! The show. Only during the last show, I lost you within ten minutes. I walked around by myself for two hours. There were a couple of girls from netball I hung out with at the end.
Hanging out at the rollercoaster... checking out the boys.....	Yes, I know you, checking out the boys. You disappear in no time. Just like last year when I lost you. You don't care about anything else when you are at the show.
Afterwards we could have something to eat together. Would you like that?	I bet I will end up eating alone.

In the end, Daisy says to Lola: "No, thanks. I always end up alone when we go to the show."

And Lola thinks: "Huh?"

They are no longer talking about an outing to the showgrounds, but about Daisy's frustration. Lola probably has some unresolved emotions too, and brings them up. Before they know it, they are having a shouting-match.

The solution is to talk it all over. To clear the air. The swerving stops naturally.

When swerving is dangerous

When we are having a chat, swerving is okay. One moment we are talking about horse riding, the next moment we are talking about dirt bikes.

But we had better be careful not to swerve in a dialogue. During a discussion, swerving is even less advisable. We are talking about one topic. We give our point of view. Jumping to another topic can cause irritation.

When we are talking, our brain fires special neurons that communicate with each other. When we listen carefully to one another, we are literally "on the same wavelength".

When we are in discussion, we are trying to convince each other. Swerving makes the conversation chaotic. It is better to resolve the topics one by one.

Swerving is super dangerous in a shouting-match. We both climb higher and higher up the communication ladder – with terrible results.

How to avoid swerving

The solution to swerving is easy. There are three steps:

1. Notice it

Next time we make a point in a conversation, we should listen carefully to the other person's reaction. Is it relevant to our point, or do they change the subject?

⋮3 steps⋮

notice it

Relax

Resolve it

2. Relax

If the other person changes the subject, we should remain calm. We will probably feel a bit irritated or angry, because:

- The person is not reacting to what we are saying, and that does not feel right. Or:

- The person has unresolved feelings towards us. This does not feel good, either.

Remain calm. Count to ten. Think. Breathe in… breathe out.

3. Resolve it

Say: "Okay, I understand you want to discuss something too. So let's go through the issues one-by-one."

If all goes well, we discuss both subjects and the air is cleared.

Whose point first?

What happens if we recognise swerving, but the other person wants to have their say first?

Of course, this is irritating because we had brought up our subject first. It is only fair that this should be discussed first.

Or is it?

There are two ways to go about this:

1. We ask for our point to be discussed first;

2. We offer to discuss the other person's point first.

Which one we discuss depends on its importance. Did the other person bring up a more important point? Then we discuss that first. If our point is more important, we discuss that first.

When we try to empathise with the other person (using our social skills), we will end up doing the right thing.

Keep in mind that we are communicating to reach a certain goal. Sometimes this is reached more easily if we give the other person some space.

Swerving off-topic will always happen. Be alert to it.

Swerving off-topic will keep happening. Be aware of this. Sometimes just noticing it is enough to give both people involved some space. That way we come to like each other again sooner.

But the danger of swerving is always there. It can pop up in the middle or at the end of a conversation. If you train yourself, it becomes second nature to recognise it.

We can often observe swerves off-topic in television series and movies. This is understandable, because to keep people's attention, TV series and movies need problems. Just put swerving off-topic in the script and a lot of problems will arise between the characters. Watching a television series is a good way of learning to recognise swerving off-topic.

Summary

In communication, people often jump from one subject to another. This is called straying or swerving off-topic. It is not a problem during a chat. But it causes problems in dialogues and discussions. And it is extremely dangerous in shouting-matches. Swerving causes a conversation to become chaotic.

It is a good idea to make sure we discuss topics one by one. That enables the conversation to go more smoothly.

14

Avoid wild words

Introduction

In the chapter about the power of words we learned that the words that we use have great impact – not only on the people around us, but also on ourselves and on our self-esteem.

The third important pitfall in communication concerns particular types of words. Enormously powerful words. They have such a negative impact that it is wise to avoid them all together – because they cause a lot of problems.

Never and always

The words "never" and "always" are often used when stating points of view and opinions. This is problematic.

- You are always angry
- You are always so irritating
- I am never allowed anything
- You never clean your room

The words "never" and "always" cause a negative emotion in the listener. This is understandable, because 99% of "never and always" statements are untrue.

This is why the other person feels anger when we use them – we are telling a lie about them. We may not be aware that that is what we are doing, but it does not make any difference to the other person.

Alternatives

A word that is similar is "constantly".

- You are constantly angry
- You are constantly away

"Constantly" is just a fancier word for "always" or "never". It is better to say "often" because this is closer to the truth.

- It seems to me you are often angry
- I believe you are often angry
- I feel you are often angry

This sounds much better than "you're always angry", or "you are constantly angry".

"You are often angry" also indicates that we are willing to help the other person. And when we use 'I think, I feel, I believe', we own what we say by adding 'I' to the sentence.

Everything, anything and nothing

Another pair of hair-raising words: "everything" and "nothing". Recognise them?

- You mess everything up;
- You always mess everything up (double whammy!);
- Nothing you say makes sense to me;
- Can't you do anything right?;
- I always have to do everything by myself (double whammy!).

These words cause strong reactions. They are untrue most of the time. And to be lied to is terrible. Only use expressions like these when they are true – or avoid them altogether.

Alternatives

It is better to use "often" or "frequently" instead. And try to use positive words instead of "nothing".

- I think you can do better;
- How can we make sure you do better?

I do not HAVE TO do anything

Another thing that drives us wild: "Have to".

- You have to listen more carefully;
- You know what you have to do?;
- You have to push yourself;
- You have to go to the family gathering.

As soon as people hear "you have to", they feel resistance. Whether the words are true or not, they cause irritation. Granted, if our room is such a pigsty that our bed has become invisible, we really do have to tidy our room. But hearing the words is still irritating.

Alternatives

We can replace "have to" with more friendly words. For example, "would you, please" or "can you, please":

- Could you please tidy your room?
- Could you please listen for a moment?

Empty conversation-killers

An empty conversation-killer is a generalisation that does not add value to the conversation. These stand in the way of an intelligent dialogue or discussion. Examples are:

- Why? Because I say so!
- It is simply a question of taste…
- You are entitled to your opinions…
- Why? Just because!

These immediately kill a conversation. There is no real comeback other than "Duh"? The person using them has probably run out of arguments. They are always a sign of weakness. Empty conversation-killers are a way of losing respect. It is best to avoid them. Try to avoid them.

Rude and empty words

There are plenty of rude and empty words and phrases. Among them:

- Get lost!
- Haven't you got a brain?
- Learn to think straight!
- You are useless!
- Piss off!

There are thousands of them. Needless to say, they do not help us reach our goals. Quite the contrary.

Always keep in mind that we are trying to attain our goals. Whether we like the other person or not, it's better to solve problems together. We both want a good result. Rude and empty words do not assist us in any way. If we use them we simply risk our relationship with the other person deteriorating further.

These words are a waste of time and energy. It is better to avoid them completely.

What if other people use rude words?

If we are alert to rude or angry words, we can ask the other person why they are using these words – what they intend to say. We can use "Do you mean that…" Yes, the good old "Do you mean that…"!

One solution for two communication pitfalls:

Example

John:
"You're always late."
Bill:
"Do you mean that I am never on time?"
John:
"Er, no, but recently you've often been late."

Or

Mother:
"You always mess things up."
You:
"Do you really mean that?"

Mother:
"No, but lately…."

Or

Daisy:
"Piss off!"
Lola:
"What do you mean? Do you want me to go away?"
Daisy:
"No, I just want us to have fun together."

When we are alert and use "Do you mean that…?" we create some space in the conversation. It gives the other person time to think about what they are saying and what goal they want to reach. It also gives us the time to think about whether there is a grain of truth in what was said.

Summary

If we are serious about reaching our goals, we want to avoid wild words. Those words do not add any value to a conversation. They only cause negativity. Do not use them at all.

If another person uses them, use "Do you mean that...?" to clarify what is going on.

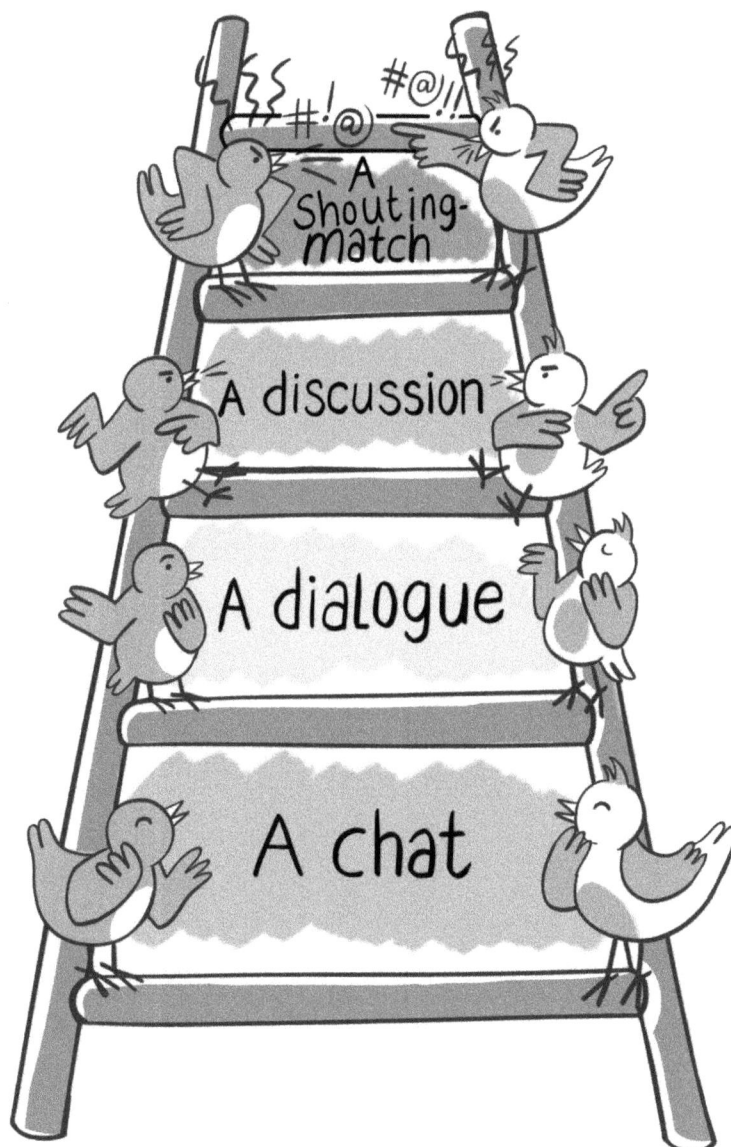

15

Don't forget the ending

Don't forget the ending

Introduction

This is the last chapter. We are well on our way to becoming communication champions. But there is just one more thing to share:

Don't forget the ending.

When we have landed in a robust discussion or even a shouting-match, we may notice that they often end quite abruptly. The participants seem just too tired to go on. So, they let it be.

This 'letting it be' can turn into days, or even weeks, or even months, of non-communication. So we need to pay close attention to the way that a conversation ends.

Why the ending is important

Movies without a real ending – aren't they annoying? They call it "having an open ending". The director leaves us hanging there. We are invited to imagine the ending ourselves. This can cause a nagging feeling. Something is not quite right, but we do not know what it is.

A discussion or a shouting-match without an ending feels wrong in a similar way. We get that nagging feeling that things are left unresolved. And this is not a movie, but real life. We just know the problem will return unexpectedly and at an inconvenient time.

This is why it is important to end a discussion or shouting-match well – so that we both know where we stand, even if the problem has not been resolved.

By ending a difficult conversation well, we avoid problems accumulating. Because if that happens, we will become irritated faster the next time we have the slightest of arguments.

A summary of possible endings

To make things easier, here is a list of the most useful endings.

Ending 1: problem solved, nobody was right or wrong

This is the easiest ending. If we have worked through all the chapters of this book, we will find that shouting-matches are unnecessary. They often arise out of misunderstanding. When we are open to other people's points of view, we are more likely to resolve things.

But it is a good idea to make sure we actually express what has happened. Something like

"Okay, this was clearly a misunderstanding. Let's move on from it."

Ending 2: To admit that we are wrong can be fun

There is no shame in admitting that we are wrong. We cannot be right all the time. Sometimes we land in a discussion just because we are in a bad mood. We do something wrong and…. Bang! We are in a shouting-match.

This is not very clever and the chances are that we will have to admit we are in the wrong. If we remain angry, it is not helping the other person – or ourselves.

In fact, admitting that we were wrong is quite a good feeling. And the other person will respect us for it. This increases our confidence.

But humans can be strange creatures. Even if they have their backs against a wall, they will still defend their opinions, even if those opinions are wrong. This kind of behaviour is a real barrier to communication. It is like being in a soccer match that ends in 5-0 for our side, then the other side says: "We won!"

It's good to avoid doing this and to notice how good it feels to admit that we were wrong.

Ending 3: Taking a break

The half-time break during a sports match is important. It often causes the side which is losing at the time to regroup. They leave the dressing room with a different attitude. They may even win. What happened in that break?

During the break, the coach and the players address all issues one-by-one. What went right and what went wrong? And more importantly: What can we do to make things better? By changing their tactics, the team ends up winning. Incredible!

We can do the same when we are in a discussion or a shouting-match. Sometimes we cannot stop. Everything has been said. But we still carry on.

What is added does not have any positive value – the only thing added is irritation. It is better to avoid this. There is nothing wrong with taking a break to allow everybody to take a breather and regroup their thoughts. The tension disappears from our bodies and we can think clearly again.

It is not a sign of weakness to suggest a break – on the contrary. We show that we are participating in the conversation and are thinking about a solution. We understand that a break is needed to reach our common goals. Other people will respect us for that.

A thirty-minute break is probably not enough. We need some time to concentrate on other things. A couple of hours is better, or a day. Remember the expression: 'Let's sleep on it.'

Ending 4: Agreeing to disagree

Sometimes the various points of view are so far removed from each other that a solution is not possible. When we have tried everything else, we can agree to disagree. This is an amazingly simple solution. There is no shame or problem involved. In the end everybody has their own set of values. That said, it does depend on the subject. The following construction will not work:

"Miss, I don't like maths. I don't want to do any more maths. I know you don't agree, so let us agree to disagree."

If we agree to disagree, it is important that we respect each other's point of view. Agreeing to disagree is not a licence to ridicule the other person's opinion.

Disagreement is actually a good thing. It shows there is diversity in the world. We are all unique, with unique opinions. This makes our life richer and we can learn from it. Who knows, we may change our opinions in the future.

Let bygones be bygones

When we have decided on an appropriate ending, that is really the end of it.

For example, if one party has admitted they were wrong, it is time to stop. We could go on forever, but that would be a waste of time and energy.

This means it's time to forgive and forget. If someone has apologised, forgive them. And more importantly: forget.

Forgetting often goes wrong – the subject is raised again in the next discussion, even if it is completely irrelevant. This is a cause of irritation.

So: let bygones be bygones.

Summary

It is important to end communication well. That does not mean we all have to agree. We can take a break before trying to solve the problem. A break helps to regroup. The next day we will see things more clearly.

Other ways of ending a conversation are to admit that we were wrong or to agree to disagree.

We can always pick up this book and review it. Who knows, we may find a good solution!

Some final words

Introduction

Intelligent communication is fun to learn. It makes our relationships better. And we get more done. That makes us feel good about ourselves. Feeling good about ourselves gives us the energy to do more. I hope you enjoyed this book.

We can train ourselves in intelligent communication every day

Because we communicate all day long, there are plenty of opportunities to get better at it. Most conversations are suitable for observing what goes right and what goes wrong.

Let's see if we can spot swerving off-topic, whether people are really listening to each other and whether they are really hearing each other. Are any assumptions being made?

People who have read this book will recognise all these aspects of communication – and they will be able to apply them in their own conversations.

Other people's conversations are a convenient way of mentally training ourselves. When we ourselves are engaged in communication, our emotions come into play and make things more complicated. When we observe others, we can get better and avoid common mistakes.

Communication is about persevering

Sometimes communication can be painful, especially with our loved ones.

When things get difficult we need to bear in mind that:

We have no choice

Communication is everywhere. We have no choice but to engage in it. That is why it is important to learn about it.

It is fun to reach goals

Let us keep in mind what we are doing it for. Everybody wants to be successful. Definitions of success may differ, but we all want to reach our goals. By communicating well, we will reach our goals sooner and more easily.

It is great to be happy

This sounds obvious of course, a truism. But still it is true, and with intelligent communication our relationships become better. That is what makes us humans happy. When our relationships are better, we feel happier.

We will get better and better

If we apply everything discussed in this book, we will get gradually better at communicating well. Not from day one — it works the same way as with dancing, maths, soccer, or netball. We need to practise, practise and practise some more.

We can practise all day, and if we do so, we will get better every day. Like any skill, these skills will become second nature once we have learned them.

Anything is possible

We have reached the end of this book.

I have a confession to make. When I was at school, I was not particularly good. Maybe I was not clever enough. Or maybe I was lazy. Maybe I was too clever. Who knows? Whatever the reason, I learned one invaluable lesson – not at school, but from my parents. They taught me that if you really want something, it can become a reality.

And that counts for you too. The secret lies in the words REALLY WANT. If you do not really want something to become a reality, it will not happen easily. The reason I say this is:

Always remember that anything is possible – whether or not you do well at school.

If you believe in something and you really want it, it can come true. No matter how big your dream is, do not let yourself be held back.

The second thing I learned from my parents was to communicate well. I am incredibly grateful for that. It meant that I became happy and reasonably successful, in spite of my mediocre school results.

I wish the same for you, from the bottom of my heart.

Paul.

For parents and teachers

Research

In writing this book, I first put my own ideas about communication on paper. I just wanted to get all the handles on communication I could think of. I also wanted to describe why we should want to communicate better.

For many years I have believed that intelligent communication is a major factor in our happiness and success. This is why we need to get better at it. Not only for our own success and happiness, but also for the success and happiness of other people.

Personal relationships are paramount in our lives, and intelligent communication is a key tool in maintaining these relationships.

Communication has been researched scientifically since the 1970s. Examples:

Interpersonal relationships are a driving factor in our lives. Most Americans report that the quality of their lives is determined by the number and quality of their interpersonal relationships (Campbell 1980)

Individuals with good relationships live longer and report less physical and psychological illness and greater satisfaction in life (Duck 1981).

The failure of interpersonal relationships has been associated with suicide (Stech, 1980), psychiatric problems (Bloom, Asher, and White, 1978), social stress (Chiriboga, 1979), and family instability (Albrecht, 1980).

Effective communication is a crucial variable in determining the success of interpersonal relationships (Alexander, 1973; Murstein 1972).

Communication is a requirement for maintenance of satisfying relationships (Alexander 1973: Cushmand and Cahn 1985; Murstein 1972, 1977).

The absence of effective communication causes relationship failure (Alexander 1973).

It all makes sense...

I think we all feel that intelligent communication makes us happier and more successful. It makes sense, doesn't it?

Intelligent communication has so many advantages:

Helping to understand people

We often do not understand why other people display certain behaviours. Most of the time, those behaviours start to make sense when we understand the motivations behind them. Intelligent communication reveals these motivations.

Helping people feels good

As soon as we know the motivations that underlie behaviour, we can analyse the motivations and the behaviour. This enables us to help. And helping makes us feel good.

Making us better at starting relationships / friendships

When we are able to understand and help others it is easier to start relationships or friendships – at the gym, a club or with our future partner. We cannot live without relationships.
The more good relationships we have, the richer our lives are.

Minimalising shouting-matches

When we can express clearly what we value and what we don't value, we decrease the chances of a shouting-match. We know better what we want and what we don't want in a relationship. And that causes us to be calmer.

Enabling us to influence situations

When we communicate better, we have better control. Not to get our way, but to be able to explain better what we stand for, what causes are important to us. This increases our chances of reaching our goals.

Making people appreciate us

When we can give sound advice, prevent disputes, solve problems and explain plans clearly using intelligent communication, we gain the respect of other people.

Helping us to relax

Nothing stresses us out like a heated argument! Whether at work, with our partner, or amongst friends, they are exhausting. Intelligent communication helps to prevent and solve problems between people. The result is that we are more relaxed.

Giving us more control

When we are able to help others, influence situations, solve problems between people and choose the right friends, we feel more in control. This makes us stronger and happier.

Enabling us to understand ourselves

Communication is, in fact, asking for feedback. Feedback can be painful. But ultimately we build a balanced self-image through feedback. Once we know our strengths and weaknesses, we feel calmer and stronger. From there we can begin to work on our weaknesses.

We get better at saying goodbye

When we understand the actions and motivations of others, we are better able to choose who we mix with. We realise that we do not have to be friends with everyone. When we choose to be with people who make us feel good, we appreciate these people even more.

Increasing the chances of the career we want

All the above benefits of intelligent communications lead to a more satisfying job, and in almost every job intelligent communication is paramount.

Increasing self-esteem

The benefits of intelligent communication also lead to better self-esteem. The more goals we reach, the better we feel about ourselves. This becomes the basis for establishing and attaining more goals, and a successful life in general.

Communication, happiness and success

I am convinced that intelligent communication leads to a happier and successful life. Most people agree with me when I ask them about it. But I'm sure you'd like some evidence.

Being happy leads to success

The correlation between happiness and success was also researched in a publication by Sonja Lyubomirsky, Laura King and Ed Diener in a bulletin of the American Psychological Society.

https://www.apa.org/pubs/journals/releases/bul-1316803.pdf

What is happiness and what is success?

These are important questions when it is being argued that intelligent communication leads to a happier and more successful life. What exactly do these concepts mean? What is happiness? There is no clear answer to that question. Happiness means different things to different people. It also differs by region, country, culture, and continent. Religion can also play a role. And being happy is not a continuous state, either.

How is happiness measured? In many ways. There are many studies regarding democracy and happiness and corruption and happiness, but not so many about small-scale happiness. For me, the elements of happiness are:

- A sense of being in control;
- Being content with oneself and one's actions;
- Being grateful for small things;
- Having a number of people who love you;
- No great need for material wealth;
- In most situations you can put yourself first; (except for the kids)
- You have enough energy to be active;
- You have confidence in yourself, and a belief that everything will turn out well in the end, even if things go downhill for a bit.

You may have other ideas, and this list is not complete anyway. But it shows how happiness is different for different people.

Being successful

And what does being successful mean? This too is difficult to pinpoint. Success, also means different things to different people. Literally it means reaching the goal that we had in mind. That goal can be small or large. Success is often associated with a high-earning job, but money is not necessarily related to success. Success can lie in sports or in volunteering.

Work forms a major part of many people's lives, so here is my own list of elements of success in the workplace:

- Passion for the job;
- The job is sufficiently challenging;
- The salary is sufficient;
- Co-workers are nice and wish each other well;
- The location is good;
- There is enough stress, but not too much;
- A good work-life balance.

Again, this will be different for different people. Some will need more money than others. For some people the location will be important, for others the work satisfaction. If your list makes you happy it means you are successful. That is the definition. And the elements may change over the course of one's life.

Good models lead to good behaviour

Children learn mostly by example. If teachers wants to teach their classes intelligent communication, they have to practise what they preach. The same counts for parents. They too have to set a good example.

This can be tricky. When teachers and parents were at school, communication as a subject was not on the curriculum. But teachers and parents have one thing in common: they want the best for the children. Fortunately, they will be in a position to give a lead to the children after reading this book.

A fortunate side-effect is that their parents and teachers will enlarge their own skills, communicate better and become happier, as well as setting a good example to their children.

Acknowledgements

Writing a book is a lot of work, and is not something that an author does alone. For this reason I would like to thank the following people. The list is in chronological order, so it shows how things developed.

Firstly, Eveline Vlasveld, Astrid Frens and Tom Paulides (all people with a passion for education) for listening to my story in December 2016 and giving feedback on the idea. Without their initial enthusiasm, the entire programme might never have been created.

Eveline, Astrid, and Tom also read the first edition of this book and gave their feedback once again. Their feedback contained important information that was incorporated into the second edition. It is wonderful that you all wanted to participate. Thank you!

Then my friend Mirjam van der Loo did a first round of corrections. I suddenly remembered where all the commas go. I might have missed some (-: But that was not all that Mirjam corrected. She took a good look at the structure too. Thank you, Mirjam.

The next person who became involved was Fleur Vooijs. She had just finished her first year of the Dutch PABO, primary school teacher training college, when she proofread the third edition. Fleur, Eveline, and I then began structuring the curriculum. I could never have done this on my own. Thank you, Fleur!

When the curriculum was still in draft form, we wanted to pilot it in a school, to experience first-hand what worked and what did not. We were able to do this with the help of the Principal Anneke van Vliet and the teacher of group 8*, Monique Reijngoud. Thank you both for trusting us!

At the beginning of the project, Eveline Vlasveld was a valuable person to exchange ideas with. As a former principal, coach for children and parents, and teacher, she has an unrivalled appreciation of the value of intelligent communication. I knew I was on the right track when I encountered her enthusiasm and feedback. Thank you, Eveline!

Two other very special people are Lilian Snijders-Loontjes and Marijne Sammels. They brough new energy to Communication is Everything at the beginning of 2019. Their knowledge of social-emotional skills lifted the project to a new level, and their passion and skills gave me the tenacity to push forward with the project. Thank you for all the energy, ladies!

And lastly, I would like to thank all the people who volunteered to read the last draft of this book: my parents; my good friends Aad Slingerland and Angela Kramers; my lovely wife, Lisette, and my daughters, Isabel and Lois. These two, of course, take me to task sometimes when we have a conversation. ("That is an assumption, Dad, you'd better avoid that next time." :-)

This book was translated by my sister in law, Suzanne Visser, for Australia, and edited by Phil Walcott. It was published for an Australian readership by the Clear Mind Press.

Lastly but certainly not least, Jonathan Smith did the final editing of the Australian version of the book. Lots of i's were dotted. Thanks ever so much, Jonathan.

Paul

www.ingramcontent.com/pod-product-compliance
Lightning Source LLC
Chambersburg PA
CBHW060957030426
42334CB00032B/3269